THE POWER
OF
GRATITUDE

Liv Larsson

www.friareliv.se

If you have not purchased this book directly from us, e-mail or call us if you wish to receive our book catalogue and newsletter.

© Copyright: Liv Larsson 2014. First published in Swedish 2011.
Original title "TACK! Uppskattning, tacksamhet och lycka som livsstil".
All rights reserved. No part of this book may be reproduced by any mechanical, photographic, or electronic process, or in the form of a photographic recording, nor may it be stored in a retrieval system, transmitted, or otherwise copied for public or private use without the written permission of the publisher. Requests for permission should be adressed to:

Friare Liv
Mjösjölidvägen 477
946 40 Svensbyn
Sweden
Phone: + 46 911 24 11 44
info@friareliv.se
www.friareliv.se/eng

Author: Liv Larsson
Translation: Liv Larsson and Birgitta Nilsson
English editing and language support: Belinda Poropudas
Proof reading: Peggy Smith
Layout: Kay Rung
Ilustrations: Vilhelm Nilsson
Cover design: Liz Tencic www.Komandå.se

ISBN: 978-91-87489-23-5 Print
ISBN: 978-91-87489-24-2 Epub

Content

Preface by the Author	7
Chapter 1 – The Many Faces of Gratitude	10
Gratitude as a Lifestyle	10
Gratitude - a Natural Consequence	11
How Gratitude Grows	13
The Gratitude Puzzle	16
Mourning and Accepting	21
Chapter 2 - Sabbath	26
Sabbath	26
Chapter 3 Appreciation Reaching its Target	32
Intention	32
High Octane Appreciation	34
Differentiate Between Observations and Interpretations	38
Enhance the Octane Level in Appreciation You Receive	40
Communication That Contributes to Gratitude	41
Appreciation á la Nonviolent Communication (NVC)	43
Receiving Appreciation	44
Appreciation Can Be Painful	47
Appreciation Junkies	51
Praise as Punishment	52
Taking Things for Granted or Forcing Gratitude - Two Sides of the Same Coin	55
Be the Change You Want to See in the World	58
Resistance to Expressing and Receiving Appreciation	61
"A Man's Praise in His Own Mouth Stinks"	63
Comparisons	64
Appreciation Missing it's Target	65
Chapter 4 – Happiness Tools	67
Happiness Comes, Happiness Goes	67

Happiness Creates Ripples on the Water	70
Money and Happiness	72
Things that Happy People do	74
Your Happiness level	74
Your Happiness Strategies - a Test and a Tool	76
Motivation	80
Chapter 5 - Welcome to the Happiness Gym	81
One Year of Gratitude	81
52 Exercises to Build Gratitude Muscles	86
Week 1 Gratitude Diary	87
Week 2 Enjoying Gratitude	89
Week 3 Appreciating Somebody Else	90
Week 4 Expressing Your Appreciation	91
Week 5 Appreciating Yourself	92
2nd Happiness Survey	93
Week 6 Gratitude Diary	94
Week 7 Doing Nothing	96
Week 8 Receiving Appreciation	98
Week 9 Asking for Appreciation	99
Week 10 Thanking the Day!	101
Week 11 Express Appreciation to Someone Else	103
3rd Happiness Survey	104
Week 12 Appreciating Yourself	105
Week 13 Quarterly Evaluation	106
Week 14 Choose what Works for You	107
Week 15 Thanking Your Food!	108
Week 16 Gratitude Over Met Needs	110
4th Happiness Survey	111
Week 17 Connecting Needs to Gratitude	112
Week 18 Who Wants Appreciation?	113
Week 19 Appreciating Your Body	115

Week 20 Emotions as Clues to Gratitude	116
Week 21 Expressing Appreciation	118
Week 22 Your Link in the Chain of Giving and Receiving	119
5th Happiness Survey	120
Week 23 Appreciating Everything You See	121
Week 24 Symbols of Gratitude	122
Week 25 Gratitude Album	123
6th Happiness Survey	123
Week 26 Evaluation – Half Way	124
Week 27 Choose an Exercise	125
Week 28 Appreciating the Person You are Today	126
Week 29 Gestures of Gratitude	128
Week 30 Appreciating a Contemporary Role Model	130
7th Happiness Survey	131
Week 31 Things That Stir Happiness & Joy in Me	132
Week 32 Heart Connection	133
Week 33 HeartMath in Action	135
Week 34 Places of Gratitude	136
Week 35 Gratitude Walk	138
Week 36 Quarterly Evaluation	139
8th Happiness Survey	140
Week 37 Choosing an Exercise	141
Week 38 Appreciating Your Body	142
Week 39 Gratitude for What You Take for Granted	143
Week 40 Appreciating Role Models	145
Week 41 Expressing Appreciation Again and Again	146
9th Happiness Survey	147
Week 42 Thanking the Senses	148
Week 43 Appreciating your Ancestors	149
Week 44 Appreciating Yourself for the Last 24 Hours	150
Week 45 Doing nothing	151

Week 46 Expressing Appreciation	152
Week 47 Happy Birthday!	153
10 th Happiness Survey	153
Week 48 Who Wants Appreciation?	154
Week 49 Appreciating Yourself	155
Week 50 A Future You Are Grateful for	156
Week 51 Expanding Your Heart –Appreciating an "Enemy"	157
Week 52 Gratitude to the Most Important Person in Your Life	158
Evaluation and the Last Happiness Survey	159
If the Fire of Motivation Fades Away	160
Thirty Days Challenge	162
Which Exercises Suit You Best?	163
Cooperation Between Heart and Brain	166
Questions and Answers About HearthMath	168
Oxford Happiness Survey	169
Thank You!	172
Litterature and References	174
About the Author	175

Preface by the Author

I clearly remember the moneybox from Sunday school. On top of it was a black boy kneeling with hands clasped in prayer. He nodded his head whenever a coin was put into the box. I had never met a person with another skin color than my own, and this boy, made to look like he came from the African continent, made an impression on me. I put my coin into the box, because I had learned that it was good to be generous and to give to those who were poor. And the boy was poor I was told. I felt embarrassed when it was my turn to put my coin in the moneybox, as it was hard for me to look at his humble nodding.

I also remember how as a child in school I was invited to eat the food on the plate with words such as, "take a bite for the poor children in Africa", "Be grateful that you have enough to eat." This made it even harder to eat and the food seemed to grow in my mouth. The double message of eating more because children in other countries suffered from famine created a short circuit in heart and brain. In retrospect, I know I was far from the only one who desperately wondered if I could send the food that I did not want to eat, to those hungry children.

Later in life I met, and was influenced by, so-called "positive thinking". You should think positive, be thankful for what you have received, and be content with being the one again carrying out the trash. If you only did it with a smile, it would rub off and soon others would also do the same, no matter whether it was about garbage, exercise or quitting smoking. And yes, it sometimes had that effect, but this superfluous positivity left a bad taste in my mouth and I longed to experience true gratitude and genuine motivation to give. These are some of the experiences that made me think of gratitude as false or complicated.

Therefore, I am grateful that for some years I have had the opportunity to immerse myself in appreciation and gratitude. It has been invaluable for me to have a test group trying out all the exercises in this book and joining me in twisting and turning the different concepts. I've had a chance to ponder the difference between "positive thinking" (based on the idea that it is precisely the fact that we are thinking positive thoughts that creates results) and focusing on what we want and working to create it. It has meant a journey where I basically have reevaluated my whole approach to gratitude and appreciation. I have gained genuine connection with gratitude for the "small things in life". This connection does not occur when I one-up myself or try to think positively to cover up for pain. It occurs when I really "am with things as they are" and see that there is much to be grateful for even in challenging times.

A person in the "test group" that during a year tried the gratitude exercises in chapter five put it like this before we started:

"The word gratitude often feels so suffocating. I perceive it as an attempt to pacify me. It brings inequality, where the one who is least important or powerful should be the one who is grateful. Whoever owns less should be grateful to receive something from those who have more."

After six months of gratitude exercises the person above, (unaware of what she had said six months earlier about the same thing) expressed herself like this:

"Gratitude brings a nice, warm feeling inside of me that I can feel for other people, without being suffocating or demanding. Absolutely wonderful!"

Another person in the group said:

"For a long time I looked up to others from below. Many times I felt completely invisible. The word gratitude is a symbol of all that. Giving up, being grateful, not being someone. Not sticking out and not asking for anything. Just swallowing and saying thank you."

And after some work with gratitude exercises the person said:
"During this time I have gained strength to deal with a difficult family situation. Expressing gratitude for what I appreciate has clarified things that for many years I have been trying to run away from."

These were two of the many confirmations I received that focusing on developing an attitude of gratitude in everyday life brings life enhancing results.

Working on this book, I have sometimes thought that I "ought to" write something more serious. Something deep that could contribute to system change, changes that might make a difference to many people, yes that would actually "save the world". At the same time I found great joy in realizing that I do not know what contributes most to a better world. The only thing I know is what gives me joy. To have trust that joy empowers me to act in a different way than when I try to do "the right thing" or what I consider "my duty". I do not want to shut my eyes to what is going on in the world, I do not want to be blind in order to be able to rejoice. I want to stand with eyes wide open for both what works and what needs to be changed.

"Don't ask what the world needs. Ask what makes you come alive, and go do it. Because what the world need, are people who have come alive."
Howard Thurman[1]

---

1 http://en.wikipedia.org/wiki/Howard Thurman hämtat 10 januari 2011.

Chapter 1 – The Many Faces of Gratitude

Gratitude as a Lifestyle

I focus on gratitude and receive more things to be grateful for. There is something spiritual about the awe that often fills me when I think of what I'm grateful for.
Carola

Expressing and receiving gratitude is like getting a shot of vitamins. It nourishes our relationships, whether we are talking about so-called romantic relationships or relationships between co-workers or friends. Gratitude makes it clear to us what is important in life and what we can say no to. Gratitude is something we can choose to experience. It engages every cell in our body.

One aspect of the gratitude I experience as almost magical is that gratitude seems to grow as it is expressed. Our brain responds to joy and we get even happier seeing another person happy.

There is a truth in the expression "shared joy is double joy". When someone expresses appreciation to us for something we have done and we take it in, it's easy to feel grateful. When we are filled with gratitude it is also easier to lift our eyes to see what others have done that we appreciate about them. There is a positive ripple effect that creates a way of life full of appreciation and gratitude, rather than one that is manipulated by emotions of duty and expectations. We are building a lifestyle that can be described as natural, resource-efficient, self-sufficient, environmentally friendly, renewable and loving.

Research on happiness claims you will be happier if you cultivate an "attitude of gratitude." It comes as no surprise to most of us that researchers have found that the people who feel most grateful are those who are happiest, most energetic and have the strongest trust that it is possible to create a better world. We are vulnerable and social beings and we like to know that we are contributing to our surrounding. When we get that information we enjoy doing even more that contributes to life.

Research also shows that the more grateful people are, the less likely they are to become depressed, neurotic or feel anxious, lonely or jealous. Some argue that they also have a better immune system and therefore stay healthier, but the research about that is less certain.

People who experience gratitude for what they have, focus more on that than on how to "buy happiness", and therefore are less greedy and have a lesser tendency to over consume.

Even if several studies have been conducted on how to elicit "gratitude reactions" we are still not sure whether grateful people actually elicit more fortunate circumstances or if they just meet what happens in their lives differently. What is clear is that grateful people experience themselves as happier and happy people feel more gratitude. What comes first, the chicken or the egg?

Reflection:
What feelings and thoughts does the word gratitude stimulate in you?

Gratitude - a Natural Consequence

Experiencing gratitude is a natural reaction when our needs are met. At least it is so if we are not distracted by judgmental thoughts somewhere along the way. Most of us have been taught a way of thinking that obstructs the natural flow of gratitude. We might, for example, think that we deserve something, and that it is no more than *right* to get what we have received, or that it is someone else's *duty* to do this for us. In other cases, we may disregard what we have got because we think that we do not *deserve* it or that it's *more than we deserve*. Yet another reason to not feel grateful is if we suspect that we have only received something from someone who has an ulterior motive in giving the gift.

And even when our gratitude is flowing, it is sometimes challenging to express it in words. It may feel challenging because we think that others do not want to hear our appreciation. For instance, when we have expressed appreciation to them before, they have seemed uneasy to hear this. They blushed and responded to what we had said with things such as, "Oh, it was nothing" or "I love you and therefore of course I would do it", "it's just my duty as a mother / father / boss / friend / co-worker "or "you deserve it". Then the appreciation gets stuck in our throats, we perhaps feel uncomfortable when we are received in that way, and the next time we feel gratitude for something, we may not want to express our appreciation.

Yet another challenge is when we ourselves have a strong longing to hear more appreciation and therefore do not really find joy in giving it to others.

To most people it is obvious that connection between people is hampered when unmet needs are not expressed, but are allowed to "smolder". But many do not see that appreciation that is not expressed also gets in the way of connection. Gratitude is there and if our appreciation is not received it might feel as if we are not seen and heard in what is important to us.

A friend of mine admired one of our mutual friends in many different ways. She was inspired by how he solved problems and how he communicated. She described him with terms like "creative, amazing and brave" but said nothing to him. She thought that she had nothing to contribute to him, which caused her to keep her distance. For several years, her unspoken appreciation was an invisible wall between them.

Then came a time when she was focused on finding more gratitude in her life and she got in touch with the needs behind the positive judgments she was making about him. It helped her realize that she wanted him to understand how much hope and inspiration he contributed to others. When she expressed how much she appreciated him and why, he was both relieved and touched. He had noticed that she kept a distance and had interpreted it to mean that she disliked him in some way.

At first she was surprised. Then she realized that of course he could not have known how much she appreciated him, as she had never told him anything. After this he was more "human" in her eyes and she finally felt confident that she "would be enough" in his company.

Reflection:
What is stopping you from experiencing more gratitude in your life?

How Gratitude Grows

I mourn every lost chance to celebrate! When the tears have washed my heart clean, I can celebrate again.
Ellen

Since human beings are social, our needs are often easier to meet in connection with other people. Even our brains respond with joy and we receive happiness signals when we see another person's happiness.[2] Happiness and joy are contagious, so when we contribute to another person's happiness we are happy ourselves.

If we want to cultivate gratitude in our lives, it is valuable to know how to nurture it, but also how to deal with what prevents it from flowing. Gratitude is so much more than saying "thank you." Gratitude means having curiosity about life. Being curious about how we can enrich life gives us energy to deal with jealousy, greed, inertia, envy, enemy images and jealousy.

Gratitude provides a degree of acceptance, but not in way that makes us give or resign from trying to enrich life. When we realize that we are free to choose our approach to life - and see the tremendous power we have to enrich our own and others' lives – it helps us to experience gratitude.

Gratitude comes out of voluntary choice; forced gratitude is not gratitude. The automatic and polite "thank you" that many children at an early age have learned by coercion is not an expression of gratitude. Real gratitude - no matter what form it takes - is a powerful antidote to wallowing in emotion and feeling sorry for oneself. Gratitude is the "memory of the heart" and certainly it is in the na-

---

2 Bauer, Joachim (2007),Varför jag känner som du känner. Natur&Kultur.

ture of gratitude to reflect both past and present. To appreciate what you are going through in the present, but also to see clearly what has led to this, creates a sort of expansion of our heart and gives us space to wonder. When we see the connection between the past and the present, the sense of context and meaning is increased.

People like Viktor Frankl and Etty Hillesum have shown that it is possible to experience gratitude and meaning even in the most challenging of situations. Both Jewish, they were suffering under the Nazi regime and managed to find meaning in the middle of that madness. Hillesum describes how she fell in love with another prisoner and how they held hands, enjoying the sunset behind the barbed wire fence in Westerbork together.[3]

Viktor Frankl's wife and parents died in a concentration camp. Still he managed to find meaning and to survive. In his book *Man's Search for Meaning*, he describes how the prisoners that managed to experience "meaning" in different ways, survived despite horrifying conditions.[4]

If you long to nourish your gratitude and want to start right away, there are several ways to do it. One is to ask for appreciation from someone and to make sure you really receive it. Another way is to express appreciation to someone else.

A third option is to look around and try to discover what you are thankful for and regularly keep a "gratitude journal" of such experiences. Furthermore, you may want to take a walk in nature and enjoy what you see, or call and express gratitude to an old friend who did something for you several years ago, or just pause a moment and take in the abundance you notice around you. Perhaps looking a child in the eyes awakens your gratitude or listening to the laughter of someone you love.

"Mudita" is a Sanskrit word that means "joy", but above all, joy at other people's happiness and success.[5] Think of the possibility that in addition to being happy when good things happen to us, you

---

[3] Goldman, Anita (2005), Guds älskarinnor: Om hängivna kvinnor i en livrädd värld. Natur&Kultur.
[4] Frank, Viktor (1980), Livet måste ha mening: erfarenheter från koncentrationslägren; logoterapins grundbegrepp. Natur & Kultur.
[5] http://en.wikipedia.org/wiki/Mudita

could as well enjoy the successes of others and thus receive a chance to be happy more of the time.

Happiness lies in your hands, and paying attention to what you are thankful about is a royal highway available to everyone. The detailed program later in this book shows how you can build your gratitude muscles over a year. But why not start now by placing a hand on your heart. The heart is where the gratitude lives. Allow yourself a moment to be touched, remembering something you are gratful for. Take a deep breath and say a slow "Thank you."

One of my favorite quotes is "I choose to stay open no matter what!" It helps me, not always - but often, to be willing to let myself be affected by what is happening to me at the moment and to marvel at what paths life has made for me.

The Gratitude Puzzle

The Whole Existence Is a Celebration

Do not worry if all the conditions for you to celebrate are not met.
If you are worried about whether those conditions are fulfilled or not,
do you think you are going to celebrate then? You're never going to
celebrate; you will die like a beggar.
So why not now?
What are you missing?
This is what I have seen:
If you can start right now, suddenly energy is flowing.
And the more you dance,
the more it flows,
and the more capable you will be to celebrate.
Osho

There are no given requirements for how and when to rejoice and celebrate. Whether we will feel grateful or not is affected by what we choose to focus on. The very realization that we are free to choose how we relate to what is going on around us, can lead to gratitude. That freedom helps us accept, wonder and to receive energy and the will power to influence what we want to change.

As humans we feel best when we can give to others and ourselves out of our own free will. Doing something out of duty, seeing it as something that we should or must do leads to losing both joy and gratitude. To think that, "I should be grateful", or to say to someone else, "You should be grateful", separates us from natural gratitude. If we do something motivated by the hope of being rewarded or to avoid being punished, it is difficult to feel genuine gratitude.

When we do things because we want to, motivated by the joy of doing it, it becomes easier to experience gratitude, both over the

outcome of the action and from the action itself. I believe in going where joy is leading us and have often been helped by a few words of Lynn McMullan.
"Joy is God's way of letting you know you are on the right path."

Some of the assumptions I have about human beings are
- People find it meaningful to give to others
- People want to contribute to cooperation with the people nearest to them
- People enjoy seeing others happy.

Sometimes these assumptions are hard to trust and I do not hold them as absolute "truths". I'd rather see that we regularly challenge them and consciously choose how we want to relate to other people.

I do not trust prayers that do not end in action. I do not trust tears that do not end in action. But I do not trust actions that do not come from prayers and tears.
Marshall Rosenberg

When we set goals and then reach them, we feel satisfied and grateful for our capacity to do so. An important part of creating happiness in your life is focusing on what you want, rather than what you do not want. It helps you to find the strength and clarity of how you want to act. During my years as a consultant and fellow human, I have often asked the question:
"What do you want?"
and often gotten the answer.
""I do not know."

In order to receive clues about what we want, we need access to our inner life; to be connected with our feelings and needs. When we know what we want, it becomes difficult to force us to do things, and therefore we can be seen as difficult. This can sometimes make it challenging to stick to what we want, because belonging and acceptance is so important to us humans. To stick to what we need and at the same time focus on how we can contribute to others getting what they need, becomes our balancing act.

The story below from Jean Liedloffs book The Continuum Concept is a beautiful example of how good it feels to be part of a context. Cesar was born in Pepes' village but was adopted and lived for a long time in town. He went through a Venezuelan school, learned to read and write, and was reared as a Venezuelan. Pepe told this story about Cesar.[6]

When Pepe was grown, he came, like many of the men of hose Guianese towns, to the upper Caroni to try his luck at diamond hunting. He was working with a group of Venezuelans when he was recognized by Mundo, chief of the Tauripans at Guayparu.

'Were you not taken to live with Jose Grande?' Mundo asked. 'I was brought up by Jose Grande,' said Cesar, according to the story.

"Then you have come back to your own people. You are a Tauripan,' said Mundo.

Whereupon Cesar, after a great deal of thought, decided that he would be better off living as an Indian than as a Venezuelan and came to Arepuchi where Pepe lived.

For five years Cesar lived with Pepe's family, marrying a pretty Tauripan woman and becoming the father of a little girl.

As Cesar did not like to work, he and his wife and daughter ate the food grown on Pepe's plantation. Cesar was delighted to find that Pepe did not expect him to clear a garden of his own or even help with the work in his. Pepe enjoyed working and since Cesar did not, the arrangement suited everyone.

Cesar's wife liked joining the other women and girls in cutting and preparing the cassava to eat, but all Cesar liked was hunting tapir and, occasionally, other game. After a couple of years he developed a taste for fishing and added his catches to those of Pepe and his two sons, who always liked to fish and who had supplied his family as generously as theirs.

Just before we arrived, Cesar decided to clear a garden of his own, and Pepe helped with every detail, from choosing the site to felling and

---

6 Liedloff, Jean (1989), The Continuum Concept". Penguin Books Ltd.

burning the trees. Pepe enjoyed it all the more because he and his friend talked and joked the whole time.

Cesar, after five years' assurance, felt that no one was pushing him into the project and was as free to enjoy working as Pepe or any other Indian.

Everyone at Arepuchi was glad, Pepe told us, because Cesar had been growing discontented and irritable. 'He wanted to make a garden of his own.' Pepe laughed, 'but he didn't know it himself!' Pepe thought it hilarious that anyone should not know that he wanted to work.

People want to contribute to each other. It is natural. But it is only when we contribute without coercion that it has real value. When that freedom of giving as well as connection is there, we experience a tremendous power within from which to act.

One thing that helped me connect to deep gratitude was when I tested the idea that human beings that help others are never fully altruistic. I came to the conclusion that we give to others because giving in ways that make others happy makes us feel good. When I embraced the thought that people are not just martyrs when they help one another, but actually get something from it themselves, a door was unlocked in my mind.

Later I realized that gratitude has a greater power to it, if it is not connected to the concepts of "I should be grateful for what I get" and "positive thinking". Gratitude is not about trying to be positive, it is a real consequence of someone doing something that enriches life.

If we change our thinking from assuming that human beings are bad or evil to seeing them as good - we are still thinking in a way that is escalating violence on our small planet. We are still using the idea of right and wrong, which means that rewards and punishment are very close at hand. With this book I want to challenge you to rethink your concepts about good or bad and about doing things that enrich life for others and ourselves.

There is a story told many times about three stonecutters.[7] They were all three occupied with the exact same task, but when they were

---

7 Edhin, Susanna (2004), Den självläkande människan. Bokförlaget Forum.

asked about what they were doing they gave different answers:

- You can see that I am cutting stone, the first one replied with an irritated voice.

- I am earning a livelihood for myself and my family, was the response of the second one.

The third stonecutter replied, - I'm building a cathedral!

Experiencing that we are part of a larger context – as the third stonecutter did – increases our level of happiness.

Another way to experience more happiness is to achieve goals we have set for ourselves, especially if they are challenging. This leads to trust in our ability. At least as long as we are not lured into thinking that it means that we are better than others or that we "are good" for having accomplished this. If we can see our ability without comparing, we can celebrate our achievements and ourselves more fully. This might also lead to genuine gratitude for what we have received that has made it possible for us to achieve what we have dreamed about.

When we know what we want to achieve and act in accordance with what we value, the most boring chores can become meaningful. I often find it boring to do grocery shopping, but when I make conscious choices in the shop I frequently am filled with gratitude. For example, I decided to the greatest extent possible to buy food that is grown with care for the environment. When I live my values in this way, grocery shopping becomes meaningful. I also have learned a trick to enjoy standing in a long queue, which I previously used to hate. After an idea from a person in one of my appreciation groups, I have started to use it as a moment to connect with all that I'm grateful for.

I often have difficulty in setting long-term goals and have thought of that as a problem. When I got the idea of paying attention to what I feel genuine gratitude for in my life - to health, to important people around me, to the opportunity I have had to write several books, it became clear that my goals were indeed being met, without me having to think of the future.

Mourning and Accepting

"We become whole-hearted to the degree that we are willing to be broken-hearted"[8]
Brené Brown

The Positive thinking movement arrived in Sweden when I was a teenager. I heard the idea as a duty to be happy and positive even though it always felt a ungrounded. When I read Barbara Ehrenreich's book *Bright-Sided*[9], some years ago it was a great relief. I became clear that there is a cultural pressure towards being positive that sometimes gets in the way of the natural flow of gratitude.

Ehrenreich describes how she told a friend that she had breast cancer. Rather than respond to her with worry or care he exclaimed cheerfully:

"What a gift! What an opportunity! Now you can find out what is truly important in your life!"

I recognize the anger that Ehrenreich expressed over being treated this way. Anger at how I see positive thinking being used to try to escape the pain and grief that exist in our lives. Anger that we are becoming less aware of what is going on in the moment because we numb ourselves with the positive attitude that "things will get better" or "this will pass and I'm sure it will turn out well".

The magical idea that you can achieve what you want, as long as you have the right mental attitude and are thinking positively makes me both worried and scared. As I see it *both* positive thinking and thinking negatively create a kind of illusion. We believe that we can understand and explain the world through how we think. As I see life, it is less about trying to figure out how we can control it, than to live and enjoy it.

---

[8] Brown, Brene (2011), Gifts Of Imperfection. Let Go of Who You Think You're Supposed to be and Embrace Who You are. Hazelden Information & Educational Services
[9] Ehrenreich Barbara (2010) Bright-Sided: How the Relentless Promotion of Positive Thinking Has Undermined America.

One winter morning he looked out of his window as he was dressing. He did not hate the winter now, for he knew that it was merely the Spring asleep, and that the flowers were resting.

From "The Selfish Giant" by Oscar Wilde[10]

I sometime try to smooth over unpleasant situations with positive, wishful thinking and to "trust the process". A conflict that is dealt with in this way may go underground and sometimes grow due to this approach. This sometimes results in an escalated conflict. Important relationships are often affected by this approach and the next time the subject of the conflict arises it usually comes with greater force.

Likewise, I sometimes worry about thinking that things are worse than they are, and suffer needlessly.

A friend of mine wrote the words below, about how gratitude can arise when we have given ourselves time to really be honest about what is going on within us and mourn instead of "pretending nothing has happened".

As long as I can remember, I have felt guilty about having such abundant access to clean water. Turning on the tap for me has been a source of guilt, hatred and despair when I thought, "I should try to be grateful for this easy access to clean water." But a few years ago I decided to stop trying to be thankful and instead to just be with the pain over what the world looks like. In my mind I thought of all the people and animals that do not have access to water and cried and cried. I cried my tears and the tap let the water out. Then something shifted inside. Now when I turn on the tap, I experience it as a minor miracle that water comes out. I am grateful to the thousands of people who were and are involved in work that makes clean water available to me and I'm still interested in ensuring that everyone gets enough clean water.

Cecilia

---

10 Wilde Oscar, Den självviske jätten. Barndomslandets klassiska sagor (1993). Bonnier Carlsen Bokförlag AB.

We cannot numb certain feelings that we do not like. When we try to numb grief, shame, guilt or disappointment, we automatically numb joy, gratitude and happiness of any kind. Mourning at depth can give us access to gratitude and joy. I love Kahil Gibran's way of portraying this in his book The Prophet.

Then a woman said, "Speak to us of Joy and Sorrow."
And he answered:
Your joy is your sorrow unmasked.
And the selfsame well from which your laughter rises was often times filled with your tears.
And how else can it be?
The deeper that sorrow carves into your being, the more joy you can contain.
Is not the cup that hold your wine the very cup that was burned in the potter's oven?
And is not the lute that soothes your spirit, the very wood that was hollowed with knives?
When you are joyous, look deep into your heart and you shall find it is only that which has given you sorrow that is giving you joy.
When you are sorrowful look again in your heart, and you shall see that in truth you are weeping for that which has been your delight.
Some of you say, "Joy is greater than sorrow," and others say, "Nay, sorrow is the greater."
But I say unto you, they are inseparable.
Together they come, and when one sits alone with you at your board, remember that the other is asleep upon your bed.
Verily you are suspended like scales between your sorrow and your joy.
Only when you are empty are you at standstill and balanced.
When the treasure-keeper lifts you to weigh his gold and his silver, needs must your joy or your sorrow rise or fall.
Kahlil Gibran[11]

---

http://www-personal.umich.edu/~jrcole/gibran/prophet/prophet.htm#Joy

When I attended my first training in the U.S. with Marshall Rosenberg, the man behind Nonviolent Communication, somebody asked me to sing in Swedish. I had begun to explore universal human needs in depth and wanted to be sure to make a choice that would meet my needs. I was quite confused on how to do this and I did not know if I would say yes to singing or not. So I asked Marshall how I could determine what would best meet my needs. He laughed and said:
"You can never know that beforehand. You simply do what you want to do or what you feel happy at the thought of doing, and then afterwards you evaluate if it met your needs or not."

It was invaluable advice that helped me connect with the freedom of accepting how we feel. I've enjoyed it many times since. It has taught me to accept the fact that I can never figure out what life will be like in the future, or whether my needs will be met. But I can learn to connect with what I want and then let the mystery of life teach me new things every day.

*"Life's not about waiting
for the storms to pass...
It's about learning to
dance in the rain."*
Vivian Greene

Being present and attentively curious about what is happening within and around us provides more pieces to the puzzle of gratitude. Further on in the book we will see that if we are willing to "take Sabbath" and every now and then pause from producing or delivering, to listen inside of us, it will strengthen our gratitude muscles.

Another piece of the puzzle is that kind of acceptance which makes us marvel at life and its gifts.

I am grateful,
- *when I get to clean up after a party - it means I have friends,*
- *for the taxes I pay - that means I have an income,*
- *that my clothes are a bit tight - it means that I have food on the table,*
- *that the lawn needs mowing and the house needs paining - it means that I have a home,*
- *for all the complaints about politicians - that means I live in a country where one is allowed to express oneself*
- *For the distant parking lot - it means I can afford a car,*
- *for my high electric bill - that means I have a warm house,*
- *For the person next to me who sings out of tune - it means I can hear,*
- *For the laundry pile on the floor - it means I have clothes to put on,*
- *for weariness and aching muscles - it means I have been able to work hard,*
- *That the alarm clock rings in the morning - it means that I have another morning to enjoy.*

Lasse Lundberg

Chapter 2 - Sabbath

Sabbath

"When we live without listening to the timing of things – when we live and work in 24 hour shifts without rest – we are on war time, mobilized for battle.
Wayne Muller[1]

Although the word "lazy" does not have a built in blame, it has become charged in our culture because we value activity and performance so highly. Calling someone "lazy", often leads to defensiveness because in most people's minds it means that they are lacking in some way, or somehow not as good as others. Similarly, to be active or ambitious (at least in most cases) has a "positive charge".

If we want to live in gratitude, it is useful to give moments of rest, mindfulness and contemplation a place in our lives. In his book Sabbath, Wayne Muller describes Sabbath as a "time reserve." He argues that we need a sacred area inside of ourselves where we can give room to a rhythm that recreates an inner balance within us. A sacred "inner space" where we can stop and be present with what is happening right now and reflect on what our life is about.

I like the idea of an internal place where we can go to remind ourselves of what is important to us and what makes us come alive. A place where we reflect on what we as humans need to thrive.

It is perhaps no coincidence that the commandment about taking a day for rest holds equal weight with the commandment "You shall not kill" in the Old Testament. In our modern lives, many of us have lost the balance between rest and activity. We rush around and try to achieve as much as possible, giving little thought to our need for rest.

In nature there is a natural rhythm that many of us seem to have forgotten. In nature rest follows activity, winter follows summer,

---

1 Muller, Wayne (1999), Sabbath Restoring the Sacred Rhythm of Rest. Bantam Doubleday Dell.

ebb follows flood, and night follows day. Similarly nature moves through our bodies in cycles through our breath and in our hearts. After every heartbeat there is a moment of rest, after each breath a quiet moment. Nature wants rest and activity to balance in a continuous eternal stream.

"There is a pervasive form of contemporary violence... and that is activism and overwork. The rush and pressure of modern life are a form, perhaps the most common form, of its innate violence.
To allow oneself to be carried away by a multitude of conflicting concerns, to surrender to too many demands, to commit oneself to too many projects, to want to help everyone in everything, is to succumb to violence.
The frenzy of our activism neutralizes our work for peace. It destroys our own inner capacity for peace.
Thomas Merton[2]

During periods when I have been very active without resting, I have later discovered that I have taken a lot for granted. Part of the driving force behind writing this book was that I noted how easy it was to just rush through my life without stopping to be grateful for what I have and what I create. Perhaps you recognize this in yourself in the idea that things can always be a little bit more perfect, get a little bit better if you just do a little bit more, stretch yourself a little bit further. We have taken over the role of creation - perhaps out of fear of discovering that we can no longer connect with the divine.

We may postpone fun until later and take it for granted that it will still be there when we "have time". But people, including children, turn a day older every day that passes and today never comes again. I have found an increasing acceptance within myself that this is so, rather than getting stressed over it. This approach supports me in choosing what things I most value in my life.

Being active is fun and meaningful in many ways and of course

---

2. Quoted in Legacy of the Heart: Spiritual Advantages of a Painful Childhood, by Wayne Muller.

not a problem in itself. The sad part is that we lose clarity and do not let activity be interspersed with rest. Like a car blasting along the highway we lose our focus on what's going on around us and we get trapped in tunnel vision. We have forgotten why we are traveling and where we are headed. When we rush like that we easily miss the moments of silence and peace that can give us clarity about what is important in life. We risk missing moments of love that can give us energy and meaning. We risk losing playfulness and the small moments in life that without any effort can fill us with meaning and energy for a long time.

It is almost as if we are poisoned by the belief that our life gains meaning only from what we do. But the rhythm between rest and activity is natural and will always make itself known. If we do not take account of this force of nature it will take its own path, sometimes in the tragic way that we become burned out or otherwise sick and thereby forced to rest. Life wants rest and activity in a never-ending stream. There the time reserve is simply open to us as soon as we stop. To trust that there is always enough time to rest is an amazing opportunity that I would like to invite you all to enjoy.

I'm inspired by how Michael Lerner, Jewish rabbi and author, describes the Sabbath[3]. He claims that everyone can benefit from celebrating Sabbath as a recurring ritual, no matter whether they call themselves religious or not. By celebrating he does not mean any particular ritual or having to follow any set rules. He describes it as more of an attitude or an approach to life.

It does not matter what day you choose, but it is often easier to celebrate Sabbath on the same day when others around you are resting or taking a break from work. It is simply a day when we actively release our focus from what is worrying us, what we want to fix or accomplish and instead focus on what we are grateful for. During Sabbath we devote attention to what works and what has been created which we are privileged to enjoy. As I understand the Sabbath, the core of it is to take time to rejoice in what we have. A moment when we no longer focus on changing or improving "creation" but where we instead focus on enjoying and celebrating its gifts.

---

3 Lerner, Michael (2000), Spirit Matters. Hampton Roads Publ. Company.

It was inspiring for me to read the list of "rules" below for the traditional Jewish Sabbath[4]. The rules may be perceived as a liberation process, rather than restrictive. Although they are modernized they reflect the collective wisdom of a people who have practiced the Sabbath over the past three thousand years. The list gave me new inspiration as to what I can do to celebrate my Sabbath in a way that really inspires me.

- Focus on pleasurable things: Eating, sex, singing, dancing, walking, playing, joking and laughing. See the grandeur of creation, read spiritual texts, listen to your inner voice, or do what is good and beautiful - all these things are on the Sabbath program.

- Do not use money or even touch it.

- Do not work or even think about work.

- Do not cook food, clean, sew, iron or perform any housework.

- Do not write; do not use the computer, telephone or other electronic gadgets.

- Do not light fires. Not even a candle. Do not turn on the light.[5]

- Do not fix or break anything. Let the world be as it is.

- Organize nothing, do not run errands. Set aside any lists.

What you do or do not do during Sabbath doesn't matter; the most important thing is what intention you set. For example, if you exercise to get better at something, you may not want to exercise at all this day. But if the purpose is to get in touch with your body and release stress, you definitely want to do it. If you paint because it helps you to enjoy the moment, it gives quality to your Sabbath. But if you notice that there is a desire to perform even when you paint, then maybe you could refrain from painting during the Sabbath just

---
[4]. Holst, Sven-Göran (red.) (2002), En rimligare värld. Libris.
[5]. I laugh a little at this because it's a bit challenging to live up to if you live in a house as I do that is heated by wood in the north of Sweden and the outdoor temperature is 25 degrees below zero!

to really get a clear distinction.[6]

When we do not take the time to rest, the "Sabbath" will finally come when we fall asleep. "God bless the inventor of sleep," Cervantes declared. People experiencing a hard time falling asleep know the gratitude that is often felt when waking up rested.

During our sleep we are charged with new energy. Moments of gratitude during the day help us release this energy. Our body has charged its batteries and gratitude helps us to unlock its powers.[7]

---

[6]. For a mini taste of the Sabbath, you can do the exercises "do nothing" and "body appreciation" in chapter five including exercises for your year of gratitude.
[7]. Interesting research on this has been made by HeartMath-Institute at www.hearthmath com

Chapter 3 Appreciation Reaching its Target

Intention

The intention behind expressing appreciation to someone affects what result it will have. There is a difference between expressing appreciation to celebrate what we have been given and to praise or approve of somebody else. When we express appreciation as a celebration the risk that the appreciation will be perceived as a manipulation or as "flattery" is minimized.

Most of us have at some time received appreciation that meant a lot to us. And many of us have felt the "quality difference" that exists between different ways of expressing appreciation.

We might have noticed that it is challenging to get energy from appreciation that is mixed with another's expectations. The power of appreciation gets lost if it is a way for them to get us to do something we do not want to do. Maybe our parents or teachers said something such as:

"You are so good at doing this - maybe you can do even more."
or
"I expect you will have excellent results in the exam today because you're so clever."

But maybe they did not have any specific expectations nor want to manipulate us. Maybe they just did the best they could with the words they found. Perhaps we made interpretations of what their intention was because we forgot to listen for their intention to celebrate. We can remind ourselves that we have the opportunity to transform something that looks like an ordinary stone into a diamond with the way we listen. For example you can respond to the sentences:

"You are so good at this - maybe you can do even more."
with:
"So you hope that if I engage myself more into this project it will be ready soon because you have seen that I usually deal with this kind of work pretty quickly? And that thought gives you some kind of relief?"

And if the answer is yes, you can still choose whether you want to say yes or no. You can choose to hear it as an expectation, a demand, a desire or a person's wish for something to happen. In the same way you can listen for the feelings and needs of a person saying:

"I expect you will have excellent results in the exam today because you're so clever."

If you want to connect with that person's intention, you might answer with something like this:

"It sounds like you are hopeful that you will be proud of me again today? Because you have confidence in my ability to deal with the math?

Or if we believe that what the person has said is an expression of needs that are not being met:

"Are you feeling a little worried and want to get more in touch with me about how I think it will go - considering how little I've been studying for this exam?"

Expressions like "Good job" that are later followed up with "Can you work overtime tonight?" can make us wary. Especially if the boss expresses praise over our effort a third time during the same week. The way it is said, and if it is said in the context of wanting us to do more, makes it easy for us to think that the praise has no value or is not genuine, and we might throw out the "baby with the bathwater."

Since many of us carry this kind of experiences, we easily become suspicious and skeptical when someone expresses appreciation even the first time they do so. We have learned to not fully take in what the person is saying, "while we wait for the other shoe to fall". Even if the other person's intention is not to make us say yes to something, we hear demands in the appreciation anyway and it influences us to not fully take in that we have actually contributed to the person.

Another common reason that we do not fully receive appreciation is that we become embarrassed in vulnerable moments when we are seen. We do not want to appear as if we "think we are something special" and say things like "Oh that was nothing"! To help others express their appreciation in a more "high-octane" way, described in the next paragraph, can help us open our hearts.

High Octane Appreciation

"Many know how to flatter, few how to appreciate."
   Greek proverb

Appreciation can be hot. It can help people understand that they have the power to enrich their own lives as well as the lives of others. The power of appreciation can therefore be scary for some people as it can change how we see others and ourselves. Appreciation can also be lukewarm and be seen as ingratiating flatter and pass unnoticed. If the appreciation has any power or not is partly due to how it is expressed, but also how it is received.

There is a big difference between approving praise and genuine appreciation. Expressing genuine appreciation has nothing to do with trying to manipulate others into saying yes to something, or even to make them think that they are okay.

When we express appreciation and clarify what someone has contributed to that has made a difference for us, it gives the person receiving the appreciation joy and energy. It's like driving into a gas station to refuel the car, no matter whether the appreciation is directed at us or at someone else. When we "refuel" we want to make sure that the fuel fits the "vehicle". We want to fill up with fuel that provides as much energy as possible while contributing to a minimum of toxic exhaust fumes.

If we want to help someone to fill his or her energy tank, a first step is to be clear about our intention with expressing the appreciation. If we do it to celebrate, we, as the person expressing appreciation, will also be filled with energy. If we express appreciation for some other reason, such as to raise someone's self-esteem, to praise them or to show our approval, the risk is that it gives little or no energy, neither to us nor to the one we express appreciation to.

When the intention behind the appreciation can be equated to inviting others to the "party" they have helped to create, it has the potential to contribute to the lives of all involved.

Express appreciation when:

- You truly celebrate what another has done.
- You feel gratitude and joy and want others to share that joy.
- You are willing to say what the other person has done and how it has affected your feelings and needs.

Don't express appreciation in order to:

- pep-talk or to encourage someone.
- try to increase anyone's self-confidence.
- in order to make someone work harder.

Nor,
- to give somebody a bad conscience because they themselves do not express appreciation.
- to show that you are a generous person who indeed sees other people.

Being clear about our intentions behind expressing appreciation will make it easier to shift the focus from what we judge as "good" or "right" to what we value and dream of. If our focus is to express how someone has contributed to what we value, need, crave and dream about, it will give them more energy than if we call them talented, kind or good. Here are some ideas on how it can be sound.

Five Steps to Creating "High-Octane Appreciation"

1. Make it clear to yourself *why* you want to express appreciation. Ask yourself if you have no other purpose than to express joy and gratitude, or to let the other person know how he or she has influenced you?

2. Transform interpretations about how someone "is" and how you judge what someone has said or done or been, into clear observations of what you have heard or seen them do.

3. Express the needs the other person has helped you to meet and what you feel when you connect to that.

4. Allow yourself to share how he or she has touched your heart in a way that captures what you want to say. Do it in a way you think he or she can really receive. What you want to convey is how he or she, through their actions have nurtured your dreams, supported you and made choices that are in line with what you value.

5. Make sure that the other person hears you. Ask him or her to repeat what they have heard you express. If you are not satisfied with the response, repeat 1-4 again, but choose other words that may be easier for the other to connect with.

6. Or, Listen for what might lie in the way of the other person's ability to hear you. Make a guess including what the other person feels and needs, to show that you understand this stimulates feelings in him or her. Then return to points 1-3

High-octane appreciation serves as an antidote to passivity and resignation. I claim that passivity and resignation are not a natural state (just look at the active play of a three-year-old child, but is culturally learned. We have learned not to get involved in other people's business, not to interfere, and that our input does not matter. We have just forgotten how incredibly powerful we are and that we actually are always affecting each other's lives. The thing to consider is how we wish that affect to be.

If we wish to counteract the passivity in others and ourselves, it is useful to distinguish between approval and appreciation that is based on the celebration of someone's actions. Praise can contribute to increased passivity, because people are motivated to do things to be praised, and if they do not get it all the time the motivation fades away. They have become dependent on a driving force fed from the outside and become insecure and doubt their own ability as soon as others are not praising them anymore.

Many parents, teachers and psychologists have undertaken the task to build the self-confidence of others. They have learned that by telling others they are skilled, beautiful, talented and lovable they can build their confidence. But getting approval seldom or never results in "great self confidence". It more often leads to people becoming appreciation junkies that only feel okay when they get approval from others.

While the intention is, of course, to contribute to building self-esteem, it has missed it's mark, for the appreciation, which provides lasting energy to others, must be based on something other than approval, compliments or praise.

One of the strongest human needs is to contribute to the enrichment of life for us and for others. We experience meaning from knowing that we matter and by seeing that what we have put our energy into is evolving into something we have dreamt of. Therefore, it gives us energy to receive information on whether what we have done has contributed to life or not. It can take the form of words, a smile or an action. It can also come in the form of reaching a specific target.

We do not need to hear that we are good, but we all need to be heard and seen as valuable. We do not need approval but we need to have a sense of belonging. We have a need to be seen and, we might have a strong desire for a certain person to see us acknowledge us but we can experience our very human need to be seen in many other ways.

And so the need is not appreciation, what we need is feedback or clarification about whether something we have done has been helpful to someone or not. We get the power to change, by finding out what does not work for others, as long as we do not hear it as a signal that something is wrong with us but as a request from someone to enrich their life.

Differentiate Between Observations and Interpretations

By now it's hopefully clear that we can contribute to others receiving more energy from our appreciation by the way we express it. Let us also look at how our listening can transform low-octane appreciation into high-octane appreciation.

Every time a child had a birthday at the preschool where my son went, the children, with the help of the pre-school teachers, wrote appreciative sentences on a card to the child who was having his or her birthday. When my son turned five, he received a birthday card that said things like: "You are kind," "He's a good friend," "You're so funny because you are doing such funny stuff when we play Superman" and "You run very fast."

When we got home he asked me to read it out loud and afterwards he was silent for a while. Then he said with a voice I perceived as sad. "You are kind and you are a good friend are on all the cards, so it does not count".

I got curious and asked, " is there some other things that apply to you then?"

"Yes, that I do funny stuff when we play Superman and that I run fast, it's about me," he said with a big smile.

Being able to make this distinction is important for the appreciation to reach the recipient. What I mean by observation is something we can measure, something we see or hear without mixing that in with if we like it or not.

What I mean by interpretations is what we think about what we see someone do and what we think their intention is by doing it. Behind interpretations different observations are hidden. It is not certain that the other person understands what difference he or she has made, if we only say that he or she is "nice" or "kind".

It is much easier for others to understand if we express our appreciation in a specific way and include exactly what we saw or heard that he or she did:

"What I mean with saying that you are so nice is that I often hear you ask how I want things, which makes me feel confident that you really care about me as well."

In another situation, the words "you are so nice" could make someone annoyed, because they hear the appreciation as false and as an attempt to manipulate them into acting differently.

Sometimes the form of an appreciation makes a big difference, as in the example of the birthday card where it was much easier for my son to hear the appreciation that was based on observations. Sometimes, however, we risk getting stuck in a form and then the intention of why we want to express our appreciation might get lost.

A friend of mine that was studying communication did not want to use static labels on his girlfriend as he believed that these words that imply evaluations – even positive ones - and get in the way of a persons growth.

Therefore he avoided calling her wonderful, amazing and beautiful. He wanted to express appreciation and what he felt, but he dropped it because he did not find the words he wanted to use.

His girlfriend expressed disappointment and frustration and was even willing to end the relationship because she did not have a sense that he appreciated her. Eventually he realized that she would rather hear labels and receive some sort of connection with his appreciation, than by not hearing anything at all.

Gratitude comes in many different forms and is expressed not only in words. Remember that words are often beautiful companions of flowers, a hug or a warm gaze.

A Japanese man visiting Sweden showed his appreciation by loudly slurping the soup and everyone around him was bewildered, disgusted and surprised. A Swedish man visiting Japan showed his appreciation by loudly slurping the soup and everyone smiled contentedly.

In the second case above, everything was relaxed and the host felt satisfied because slurping in Japanese culture is seen as an expression of appreciation. So how to express gratitude can vary from culture to culture and person to person and may need to be adjusted to fully achieve its goal in certain situations. But the intention to celebrate can be the same even if the form is changed.

Enhance the Octane Level in Appreciation You Receive

1. Remind yourself that behind every interpretation there are observations. Ask the other person or guess what it is that he or she has seen you do that they have been interpreting as "good," "smart," or "kind".

2. Remind yourself that behind all interpretations there are feelings. Guess what the other person might be feeling. Connecting to their feeling will help your understand what he or she values. In this way the appreciation becomes a confirmation that you have contributed to his or her well-being.

3. If you want, you can ask the person if you have grasped what he or she has observed by asking: "Was it when you heard me say X?", Or "Was it when you saw me doing Y?"

4. You can also make a guess of not only what the other person is feeling but what need of theirs has been met by what you did or said. If you feel uncomfortable or worry about being irritating with posing questions - remember that the other person wants you to understand his or her appreciation. When you show that you really want to understand it, it helps him or her to feel heard. It can increase the joy of being able to contribute, and of connection.

5. Take your time to find out how what you've said or done has influenced the other person. Fully perceive what he or she has experienced through this and notice how that makes you feel. Express this to the other person.

Communication That Contributes to Gratitude

Compassion is the human expression of abundance. We are filled with an emotion that is so big that it blasts the ego boundaries.
Hildegaard av Bingen[1]

When I first encountered Nonviolent Communication (NVC), the first thing that caught my interest was the way of looking at the difference between appreciation and praise, compliments or approval.

The clarity about how our language can stimulate people's willingness to contribute to other or not, fascinated me. I was amazed to realize how compassion was influenced by the way we think and communicate. I enjoyed finding practical tools to support deep joy and to receive skills to create an attitude of gratitude in my life.

For a long time I explored the idea that when our needs are met, gratitude is a natural reaction. Again and again I discovered how appreciation reminds people of the power they have to contribute to others in meeting their human needs.

In situations where I had previously been content with "it's too wonderful to describe in words," I now often express words for the feelings these situations stimulate in me. I enjoy connecting more deeply to the needs that were met. By stating clear observations about what had actually happened, my joy increased by strengthening my connection to other people. I can now invite them to share my experiences in a different way than I had before. I found words to show people that what they said or did mattered to me.

[1] Härdelin, Alf (2005), Hildegard av Bingen, helgon.

The purpose of NVC can be described as the creation of a quality of connection that brings to life the longing to find ways to have more needs met. It is an approach in which everyone's needs are valued. Mutual respect and autonomy are key concepts as they are needed both when we want to achieve efficient collaboration and when we want to solve conflicts in an effective way.

Marshall Rosenberg, the man behind NVC, wanted to understand how it was that some people took to violence in a challenging situation, while others could relate compassionately in similar situations. He found the explanation in the way we think and the way we communicate. I have formulated some assumptions on how people can keep connected to their compassion through these four points.

1. Connection between people will happen more easily if we assume that everything humans do, we do with the intention of meeting our universal needs.

2. It is easier to connect to other people if we assume that they want to contribute to us.

3. It is more likely that we will find a joy in contributing if we feel free to do so.

4. When we express gratitude to someone, it will be easier for that person to take in our appreciation, if we clarify which of our needs were met.

Appreciation á la Nonviolent Communication (NVC)

In expressing appreciation with the inspiration of NVC we can distinguish three components.

1) The actions that have contributed to our well-being.

2) The particular needs of ours that have been met.

3) The feelings stimulated by the fulfillment of those needs.

The order may vary. Sometimes all three components can be conveyed through a smile or a simple "Thank you." When we want to be sure that the appreciation will be received, it is valuable to learn to verbally express all three.

Here is an example from Marshall Rosenberg's book *Nonviolent Communication, a Language for Life"*, in which he makes sure to get appreciation in a way that contributes to him.[2]

Participant: (approaching me after a workshop) Marshall, you're brilliant!

MBR: I'm not able to get as much out of your appreciation as I would like.

Participant: Why, what do you mean?

MBR: In my lifetime I've been called a multitude of names, yet I can't recall seriously learning anything by being told what I am. I'd like to learn from your appreciation and enjoy it, but I would need more information.

---

[2] MBR=Marshall B Rosenberg

Participant: Like what?

MBR: First, I'd like to know what I said or did that made life more wonderful for you.

Participant: Well, you're so intelligent.

MBR: I'm afraid you've just given me another judgment that still leaves me wondering what I did that made life more wonderful for you.

Participant: (thinks for a while, then points to notes she had taken during the workshop) Look at these two places. It was these two things you said.

MBR: Ah, so it's my saying those two things that you appreciate.

Participant: Yes.

MBR: Next, I'd like to know how you feel in conjunction to my having said those two things.

Participant: Hopeful and relieved.

MBR: And now I'd like to know what needs of yours were fulfilled by my saying those two things.[3]

Receiving Appreciation

Marshall Marshall Rosenberg helped me understand the importance of being able to receive appreciation. At a training session, we did an exercise around expressing appreciation to someone in the group.

As the exercise went on and no one in the group expressed any

---

[3] Rosenberg, Marshall (2007), Nonviolent Communication, a language for life. Puddle Dancer Press.

appreciation to me, frustration was growing more and more within me. I realized that I could ask for appreciation, but as soon as I was about to open my mouth a cascade of arguments came into my head about why I should not do so. Thoughts like "I have not contributed to anyone so I deserve no appreciation", which grew into, "I'm not interesting enough" and eventually to "Nobody likes me." Hand sweat increased as my heart rate increased and the thoughts spun faster and faster. In the end, I was so overwhelmed and entangled in my own thoughts and attempts to defend myself from my physical discomfort that I asked Marshall for support to handle it. He responded with a simple sentence that has helped me many times since:

"*To always be the one giving is also to be part of domination.*"

My self-critical thoughts and physical discomfort at once were shifted into tears. I cried and realized how much I had always valued independence and being self-sufficient. Only then did I also realize that it had been at the expense of connection with others. It was replaced by memories of how many times it had hurt me when my mother had waved away my appreciation with an "oh". She contributed so much to me, but it was also easy to think that I did not matter, as she seemed to need nothing from me. The pain increased when I realized how often I had chosen a similar attitude and how lonely it had made me: "I don't need appreciation, I know that I'm ok."

I was now ready to ask for appreciation from the group, although I felt extremely vulnerable. Somehow I was supported by the idea that from the womb of vulnerability creativity, joy and togetherness are born. I realized that to really connect, I needed to be willing to really be seen at this vulnerable point.

It was the first time I could really comprehend that appreciation was about how I had affected others and not about how good or talented I was. Their appreciation was an invitation to a celebration of something I had contributed to. At the same time it helped me relax, realizing that mostly it was about how they had experienced the situation and less about me. Realizing that one of the most important outcomes of giving and receiving appreciation is that it becomes a "proof" that we are linked together and that we have the power to contribute to each other, I cried even more. But this time I cried out of relief and a strong sense of belonging.

This was an important shift for me. Until that moment I had interpreted asking for appreciation as a sign of dependence and even weakness. When I saw the difference in depth between celebration and approval a third way was opened. I saw that my willingness both to ask for appreciation and to actually receive it could be seen as a sign that I'm willing to accept my mutual dependence on others. Besides, I was now more prepared to handle the situation if no one had any appreciation they wanted to express to me at the time. The important thing was to hear *how* I had affected others and to be able to relate to them, not that I was myself great or even okay.

I benefited from that experience when I was a trainer a few years later and a female participant asked the question:

"What can I do to avoid feeling like a beggar when I ask for appreciation?"

With some support, she realized that she actually gave others a chance to meet their need to contribute if she listened to their appreciation.

Think of an appreciation that would make you dance from joy?
Who would you want it from?
What makes it valuable?
What are you waiting for? Why not ask for it right now?

Another thing that can help me receive appreciation is to ask myself what I have received that has made it possible for me to give to others. It reminds me that I am in mutual interdependence, which makes it easier for me to remember that I, and others, possess the power to make a difference for each other.

What have you received that has made it possible for you to give what you have received appreciation for?

Appreciation Can Be Painful

For those of us who have strong "inner critics," receiving appreciation can sometimes feel quite painful. At the same time as we hear the appreciation our inner critics scream, "I'm not worthy of this," "If she only knew how I really am." Or the criticism is turned outward "Do not trust what she says, she just lies, she just wants to manipulate you."

Maybe we have previously relied on what someone has said and then became injured. We might have received recognition and praise that has since turned into criticism and demands.

Compliments and praise might lead to thinking that others have certain expectations of you. If someone says you're smart, you might experience it as flattering or supportive. After a couple of weeks however the word smart might feel threatening, because you think you will soon have to say something clever to that person again. Every sign of you not being all that smart haunts you and you will easily get stressed out, which rarely leads to anybody appearing intelligent. This is one of the things that make it so valuable to link appreciation to the observations of specific behaviors, and to the needs that have been satisfied. We can do that both when we express appreciation and when we hear appreciation from others. Avoiding focusing on what someone *is*, and instead focus on what they *do* that helps you meet your needs.

Instead of telling someone:

You are always so kind and thoughtful, we can say:

That time when I came to work after my sick leave and found a bouquet of flowers on my table, I was so moved! It helped me to feel welcome and safe in coming back.

Many people have learnt to listen for an evaluation or approval when they hear appreciation. So even if we try to express ourselves with a more process oriented language that describes how our needs have been satisfied at a specific moment, the other person might hear it as if we're talking about how they *are*. We don't have the power to decide how someone hears what we say, but we have power over how we express ourselves and of our intention with what we are saying.

When I lead a workshop and present this idea about not focusing on what somebody *is*, but on telling him or her what they have done that has helped us, there is often someone who reacts with irritation.

They have learned how important it is to be seen without having to perform, and therefore hear what I say as a proposal that we show our appreciation and love only when someone has done something special. Here I often take the opportunity to show that appreciation - just because it is specific – is not necessarily based on something the other person has done. I usually give some examples of this kind of appreciation.

To a child: *When I look at your smile and hear the sound of your laughter I get all warm and feel so much love.*

To a beloved: *When I wake up and the first thing I feel is your body near mine, I'm filled with joy because I experience such strong belonging.*

To a friend: *Although I'm sad when you said no to meeting me this evening, I also want you to know that I appreciate having a friend who does not say yes when she wants to say no.*

What is it that makes it difficult for some of us to receive appreciation? And what can we do to be heard properly in our gratitude if the other person resists it? One of my friends wrote to me:

I feel so frustrated, heartbroken and sad ... I have again tried to give my beloved appreciation today, but I did not reach him, he never seems to receive my appreciation. I really want him to hear how much he helps me and how he does it - or to get in touch with what is in the way, but I do not know how?

My friend saw no sign of her lover receiving what she said when she expressed her gratitude. Later she understood that he had learned that "you should not magnify yourself and not think you are special in any way." Any attempt my friend did to express appreciation activated this inner message.

There was a beautiful intent behind his thoughts. He wanted to be sure that he stayed human and that he saw everyone as having "equal value". But with that approach, he missed hearing his girlfriend and that she actually wanted to be received in how much he meant to her. He also missed receiving information that would most probably have nurtured him.

It is painful not to be heard, no matter whether we express what we appreciate or things we do not appreciate. If someone does not receive our appreciation, there are several things we can do:

We can pay attention to whether we have been clear about our observations or not. Have we given information about what we have observed, and not about how we have interpreted what we saw? Have we told exactly what the other person has said or done that has made a difference for us? It is often easier for others to receive appreciation when we simply tell them what we have seen them do or quote what we've heard them say.

Another option is trying to understand the needs behind thoughts like, "you should not boast". They may come from the person's need for acceptance or community, or perhaps from needs to contribute to balance and mutuality.

My friend in the example above, tried to meet the doubt of her beloved one with:

"Is it so that what I say sounds very strong and you want to be sure that it is consistent with how things really are for me?"

He said yes, so she continued gently.

"Do you mean you want to be sure that you will be seen for how it is and not because you think you are better than anyone else?"

After having listened to him in that way for a while, she said. *"I feel sad when you say you do not seem to receive my appreciation, because I want to be heard in my gratitude for having you in my life. When we share it is so important to me - how is it for you to hear this?"*

Slowly, slowly they came closer and she finally felt heard. By then they both were in tears and realized that they frequently talked past one another in such a way that even appreciation could make a distance between them.

I would like to quote the text below as it highlights the habit of thinking that gets in the way of celebration in a way I find really beautiful.[4]

Our deepest fear is not that we are
inadequate. Our deepest fear is that we are
powerful beyond measure.

It is our light, not our darkness, that
frightens us. You are a child of God. Your
playing small doesn't serve the world.

There's nothing enlightened about
shrinking so that other people won't feel
insecure around you.

We were born to make manifest the glory of
God that is within us. It's not just in some
of us, it is in everyone.

And as we let our own light shine, we
unconsciously give other people permission
to do the same.

As we are liberated from our fear, our
Presence automatically liberates us.

---

4 Rosenberg, Marshall (2000) Nonviolent Communication, A Language of Compassion, Puddle Dancer Press. [Often said to have been quoted in a speech by Nelson Mandela. The source is Return to Love by Marianne Williamson, Harper Collins, 1992. —Peter McLaughlin]

Appreciation Junkies

Many of us learned early on that we are okay when someone else likes what we do and accepts it. This is especially so if that someone has the power to "accept us" such as a teacher or a parent. This scares me a bit because this way of thinking makes us easy to control. We become puppets if we can only see ourselves as okay when authority sees us as such.

When we are guided by the desire to be rewarded, we risk giving up things we value. We become dependent on always getting something from outside of ourselves to prove our value. Here the understanding that appreciation is not a need becomes important.

On the other hand, we have a need to contribute and also a need of connection with our surroundings and further a need to receive feedback in order to understand in what ways we contribute to others - or not.

"She has a great need of approval" or "He's doing it just to be seen" are typical ways to imply that there is something wrong with someone's behavior. And instead of seeing their need to be seen, we judge and analyze them and imply that they should stop seeking confirmation. Instead, we can realize that they probably have grown up in a tradition of thinking that is based on right and wrong, approval or rejection, just as we have.

We all have a need to be seen. And it is easy to see that it can become destructive when someone is looking for external confirmation in certain ways and as the only way to feel okay. They, most probably, have not learned to fill their own "storerooms of appreciation" or to ask others for information in a way that makes a difference for them. Maybe they have received a lot of praise and approval but nothing that has helped them to fully connect with their power to contribute. So the energy of the appreciation (what I refer to as the Octane level) lasted a very short time and they need to go out looking for more.

If we see and value the human need to be seen, we can be of help in handling this need in a way that is not based on getting others approval.

Praise as Punishment

Many studies show that production increases when you give someone in a workplace or in a learning situation, praise, or any kind of reward or bonus. The surveys also show that even if the rewards last for a longer time the increase in production will only be temporary. Then you are back at the same production rate again, or at an even lower level than before. How come?

In his book Punished by Rewards, Alfie Kohn reports on a large number of studies on rewards and praise and how they affect us.[5] Among other things, in many of the studies there is evidence that if you praise children who willingly share something, for instance candies, with others, the child will be less willing to share in the future, at least as long as there are no adults nearby. It seems that the joy of giving is lost as soon as there is coercion, reward or thinking in terms of "deserving".

"If I do this, I get this" can lead to people, young and old, who did something out of pure joy to start seeing it as his or her "duty" or a chance to be rewarded. This is where corruption, fake smiles, and dishonesty begin. When I am an "appreciation junkie" I do things I otherwise would not have done and that I would rather not do. If I act long enough with that kind of driving force, pleasure often drops and with it the motivation to do something or contribute. Inspired by Kohn, I have summarized in a few points why praise can influence people to underachieve:

1. Praise makes it difficult for us to know which needs we help others to meet. Therefore our motivation decreases, as people like to help others if they see what effect it has. When others just say they think we are good, we get information about what they think is good or bad, but not about what they feel or need and how we play a part in that.

2. If we get credit for something that is not difficult for us, it can

---

[5] Kohn, Alfie (1999), Punished by Rewards, The Trouble with Gold Stars, Incentive Plans, A's, Praise, and Other Bribes. Houghton Mifflin.

make us think that others do not believe we are competent, intelligent or knowledgeable. The other person seems to have assumed that we would fail and was pleasantly surprised that we succeeded in what we see as a not particularly difficult task. Opposed to how it was meant, it can lead to us using less effort next time, because we assume that others do not see our full potential anyhow.

3. Being called "good", "nice" or "smart" can be perceived as an expectation that you will continue to accomplish. It can also easily be understood as a hidden agenda held by others: they praise us with the intention to give us more assignments: *"You are great. If you can do all this, you can probably do some more."*

Several winners of the Nobel Prize have suffered "writer's block" after the attention they have received.[6] Many authors that have written a very successful book have experienced it as well. The block is based on thoughts like:
"Now, my next book is expected to be even better than the first and I can not manage to do that."

Their motivation is now based on a desire for external confirmation rather than on the desire to write and express themselves. The motivation has been "kidnapped" by the praise and the "positive" labels.

4. If we have been highly praised by a particular person, it is easy to want to avoid being criticized by that particular person. A big downfall can occur if we see ourselves sitting on a pedestal built of praise and approval. The words from my teacher (who had always praised me as a "good example of nice behavior" until then) still sting when I remember being told in third grade:
"I did not expect that from you, Liv".

---

6 http://www.svd.se/kulturnoje/nyheter/ar-priset-slutet-pa-karriaren_5438545.svd Hämtat 9 November 2010.

I was eight years old and wanted to sink through the earth. She might as well have stuck a knife into my heart. Until then, she had been my queen, but this made me never want to get close to her again. After that when she tried to compliment me for something I had done, I avoided listening, because I was afraid that there were expectations behind her words. I also took any opportunity to show that she was wrong in her appreciation of my behavior.

5. When we praise someone in an approving way, there is a risk that we help to make them dependent on praise to feel okay. Their motivation for doing something turns into a chance to be appreciated. In this way, they easily can be controlled by anyone who is willing to approve of them and give them the praise they crave.

My friend (see page 48) who found it difficult to reach her partner for some time felt that she was successful in her appreciation. But after some time it appeared quite impossible for her to reach him with her appreciation any longer. The more she tried to tell him what she appreciated, the more he seemed to back off. Although she tried in every possible way to reach him, according to her, it was "like walking into a wall." Neither he nor she saw any way out of this; he only knew that he felt a vague but strong discomfort when she told him what she appreciated in their connection. One day he realized that he associated both her appreciation and her desire to get close, to a previous situation that he had experienced as traumatic. He had for some years been "stalked" by a woman he had a brief relationship with. This woman had sent him a constant stream of text messages, called and visited him at all hours, against his will. Any sign that my friend could end up acting in the same way made him want to retreat.

Taking Things for Granted or Forcing Gratitude - Two Sides of the Same Coin

After all this time
the sun never says to the earth "you owe me"
Look what that kind of love does
It lights the whole sky
Hafez[7]

A "thank you" tastes best when it is said voluntarily and as a unique expression. When we say a "thanks" in order to be polite or because it is expected, we can trace it backwards and get to the core of the gratitude.

A person who can listen with empathy can grind the dullest grey stone into a diamond. Someone who can listen for needs can choose to hear what the needs are behind the appreciation that is expressed, in whatever form it has. But it can be a challenge to hear a thank you or an appreciation that seems to come more out of duty, expectations or a hidden agenda than from genuine gratitude and celebration.

I don't think many of us like to say "thank you" when we think it is expected of us. Maybe it comes from the drilling we received during childhood in saying "thank you" as soon as you have received something from an adult. This was asked of us, of course, without the person who demanded it asking us whether we really felt grateful.

When my son was about three years old, it became clear that people began to expect this "thank you" from him. Until then, I had seen people give to him without expressing any expectation of being thanked. Now I found him more and more frequently in what ap-

---

7 Hafez.(2006) Poems of Hafez. Ibex Publishers.

pears to be a blackmail situation, where the adults hold something in front of him and say:
"If you say thank you, you will get it."

At other times a person would ask, right after giving something:
"Are you not going to say thank you?"

We experience joy in hearing others' appreciation because it is an acknowledgment that we have used our power to do something that has had meaning. We can get this confirmation in several different ways. In these situations, I usually ask my son if he wants to say thank you when he has received something. Those who ask for a "thank you", of course, want to know if what they have given was a gift for him. They can get this information by his saying "thank you" but also by observing how keen and curious he is about the gift. Most often he says thank you and sometimes not. In fact, he is often so busy studying what he has just received, that he simply does not remember to say thank you. Anyone that knows how to look for that appreciation will see it in his body language at these moments.

When "should" and "deserve" are mixed into the appreciation, they risk "hiding" the source of the gratitude. If I want to give only provided the other person shows gratitude, I might better ask myself if I really want to give. If someone does not want to say thank you, it may be because he or she does not feel grateful and then it is, at least for me, more valuable information than the obedient "thank you". Sure I like to be seen in my intention to give, but in that case I'll have to be clear about that or I will suffer.

Now we have seen that one of the things that get in the way of genuine gratitude is to think that we should be more grateful. The other side of the coin is to take things for granted, just assuming that I will get everything I want. This is numbing our experience of gratitude and can easily kill our marveling.

Our great gift of being able to adapt gives us the ability to accept new things in our lives and might also help us endure challenging situations. But this so called hedonistic adaptation[8] plays tricks on

---

8 Lyubomirsky, Sonja (2008), The How of Happiness. A Scientific Approach to Getting the Life You

us when we are no longer happy about having something that we were really longing for some time ago. Once we have become accustomed to our new car, being married or living in a big house, we do not get as much joy out of it.

On a visit to Japan, I was part of a traditional tea ceremony. During such a ceremony, the tea is both boiled and drunk with a special presence and focus. Part of the ceremony involves carefully observing the teacup you have drunk from. You must bow before it and appreciate it. A "dead object", a teacup - something I use every day when I want to drink tea! But when I bowed to the cup I was filled with an unexpectedly deep gratitude! It became clear that cups help me drink hot tea every day. Thanks to teacups I have enjoyed thousands of liters of tea and this time I got a great reminder to thank them for their support. At the same moment I felt gratitude for the cup, I connected to gratitude with those who had created the cup, to those who had grown the tea, and to those who had prepared it. When I allowed myself to pause with the gratitude of these things, I became aware of many other areas in my life where I had support that I so often took for granted. Gratitude put light on things that I otherwise would not have seen, and I was amazed that such a simple thing could stimulate all this.

Some of my friends in Poland recognized themselves when I told them about this. They told me that 30 years ago they waited quite contently in a queue for a whole day to get a ticket for a concert with the Warsaw Philharmonic. And how they are now dissatisfied and whine about how they could have used the time for other things, if they have to wait only half an hour for something.

Want. Penguin Putnam Inc.

Be the Change You Want to See in the World

"Honesty and transparency make you vulnerable. Be honest and transparent anyway."
Mother Theresa

Meister Eckhart suggested that, if we want to pray only a single prayer in our lives, let it be "Thanks." When I am grateful for something, it becomes clear to me what I value and want to nourish. Gratitude also becomes a tool for setting goals.

Focusing on what we value and trying to "be the change we want to see in the world", gives us an approach to the world, different from when we are satisfied only when reaching our own goals. When we see other people being happy it is also easier for us to enjoy our happiness.

If we act from lack thinking or from the idea that the good life is to "defeat the bad," we risk losing power. To focus on what we dream about and on what is important for us, gives us another incentive then when we focus on what we see as wrong or bad.

Before any of you start thinking that I'm talking about some kind of naive, positive, magical thinking, I want to pause for a moment. What I'm talking about is to not close our eyes to what we dislike. What I'm talking about is that when we pay attention only to what we think is wrong and bad and things that should be changed in the world, we will not see what is already being done to create a better world and what is already working. Then it is easy to cultivate beliefs that people do not wish each other well, that they are greedy, lazy or selfish, and our willingness to contribute might diminish. On the contrary, I believe that our will to act grows when we remind our self of all the little things that are continuously taking place on the planet where people enjoy supporting others.

The belief that we need to do something "big " makes us blind to the huge number of people who are at every moment, all around the planet, doing things that are in line with what I call "a better world". When only "big things count" I can never do enough and if I don't even try, it will never happen. When I notice these thoughts, I realize that I have returned to the myth that I'm the only one who can and wants to make a difference and that I need to take a closer look at how I view other people.

I've written it before, but this is worth repeating! Expressing appreciation reminds people about the power they have to contribute to life. People love to contribute (although sometimes they may have forgotten how good it feels or how to do it).

In some cultures, expressing appreciation is a basic foundation of how to create long-lasting connections 10.

People believe that punishment is not the best way to help someone realize that they have done something that has hurt others. Instead they believe that if someone has done something that has hurt someone else, it is because they have lost connection to the very human need to enjoy contributing. Punishment does not help people remember how sweet is feels to contribute and so that source of energy and directions gets lost.[9].

In this life we cannot do great things but we can do small things with great love.[10]
Mother Theresa

When I have been stuck in despair about not doing enough, I have often benefited from the above words of Mother Theresa. It's easy to get caught up in the belief that it is only when we do what we call "big things" that is worthwhile. When we think that way, it is easy to miss that people are all the time helping to create a "better world".

I have often had huge expectations of myself being able to solve the problems of the world on my own. When I realized how self-centered that way of thinking was, I felt both relieved and a bit

---
9 Benedict, Ruth (2006), Patterns of Culture. Mariner Books
10 http://www.twice.se/moder_theresa.html. Hämtat 10 februari 2010.

ashamed. There is a story about a boy who was saving starfish that have been stuck on the beach. When his father questioned him as to what was the use in saving one or two when thousands were left drying and dying in the sun, the boy lifted one starfish, looked at it and said:

"For this one daddy, for this one, it does matter!"

In the mid 80s I had the privilege to work with Mother Teresa and the nuns who, under her leadership, had created several shelters for homeless people in Calcutta. It was a meaningful time as I daily saw people living what I call the essence of love. With limited resources, but with great presence and love, the nuns, together with the help of volunteers, day after day helped with little everyday things for many people. Homeless people were able to sleep and have a shower in one of the shelters; street kids got their wounds taken care of, and many servings of rice were offered to those who were hungry.

Some of the time, I felt restless as I was focusing on what I perceived as us not doing enough. I thought what we did was of no importance because it had no lasting value; it didn't influence the powers that be or the crazy social system. And it was partly true. But it also made me blind to the fact that for this woman, this man and this child, what we did was no small thing; it was a matter of life and death. It was a moment when they experienced love, warmth and care and many time the will to live was lit in their eyes again. Gradually my ambitious and action driven parts melted away and gave room for compassion and for more joy in my giving. I slowly realized that these actions are also a part of creating a view on human being that says that human beings enjoy contributing to others. And this is equally important as changing the systems in my view.

I see value in the type of work I describe above; because it gives us examples of how humans care about each other. We love to contribute and support one another. At the same time, I believe we need to do more than help one individual after the other, if we are to survive on this planet. Parallel to ensuring that people are okay, I dream of social systems being transformed to become more and more life serving.

I believe in the idea that "happy people are difficult to dominate". When we are genuinely happy, we want everybody else to be so as well. We do not become dependent on others' approval and can promote the changes we would dance for joy at seeing. And we can rejoice at carrying our own "power station" with us wherever we go.

Resistance to Expressing and Receiving Appreciation

Reflect for a moment about what might be in the way for you to express any appreciation you feel. Both in general and with specific people at a specific time.

A common reason not to express appreciation is feeling embarrassed or afraid of not being received. It may also be because you do not know how to express yourselves, or because the other person does not seem to want to hear appreciation. Maybe you want to wait until it "feels spontaneous". But just waiting rarely makes things feel more natural or spontaneous. Sometimes the idea of expressing appreciation to somebody evokes a longing to receive appreciation yourself. This can make it challenging for us to express ourselves.

No matter what you say to yourself about why you do not want or dare to express appreciation right now, I would suggest that you avoid it in an attempt to meet needs. Perhaps the need for authenticity, need for respect or concern for the recipient. Take a moment to get in touch with the needs you think will be met if you express appreciation to someone. Once you have connected to these needs, ask yourself if there is any way you can change the expression of that appreciation. You are looking for a way that would also meet the need for authenticity or respect (or whatever you found was holding your back). I have often realized that although I think that the appreciation is not absolutely important to express (maybe some time has passed since the thing I appreciate happened) it becomes real the moment I express it. And the experience is that others are hearing my appreciation in the present moment even if it is about something that happened some time ago.

"There is something I have been thinking of many times. It is something I heard you say at least five years ago. And it is still dear to me. Do you want to hear it?"

At one point, I asked my mother, who often "waved away" appreciation, if she wanted me to refrain from expressing appreciation. After some thought, she replied:

"No, it's worth it. Sure at the moment I get embarrassed, but your appreciation fuels me for a long time!"

Another thing that is in the way of both receiving and giving appreciation is static language and labels. The following story helped me understand that I was much more influenced by this type of thinking than I had imagined.

A woman came up to me as I was in a supermarket, about to pay for my food. She expressed appreciation for the food choices I had made, that I had chosen fair trade items, and ecologically and locally grown foods. At first I was very happy and soaked up the appreciation. But then I noticed she smelled of alcohol and immediately the appreciation became worth less.

At first I was sad to discover this censorious and judgmental autopilot in me. But it also helped me to become aware of how important the need for trust and authenticity was for me. I wanted to be able to trust that she really meant what she had said and my judgment of her came in the way of that. When I realized I wanted to experience trust, and that my judgment created a wall between us, it was easier to receive her appreciation and to see the warmth of her gaze again.

You can practice receiving appreciation in this was by doing the week nine exercise - "Asking for appreciation".

"A Man's Praise in His Own Mouth Stinks"

For several days several internal critics had had a party in my head. I was to hold a workshop and did not know how I would find the strength to do it. Over the previous days I had spoken with friends that I normally received support from, but nothing seemed to help. Then I remembered the incident I describe under the heading "Receiving appreciation". (Page 98) So I called another friend and asked - not to be heard this time - but to hear three things that he appreciated that I had done in the 15 years we had known each other. He told me and I felt my heart opening and I cried. Through his appreciation I was reminded that I can do things that really support others and I then received the energy to do the workshop.

A few days later I got some more insights. Two weeks earlier I had done something I was very proud of. But I had not shared it with anyone, not openly rejoiced, remaining quiet under the proverb "A man's praise in his own mouth stinks." I discovered that when I don't follow my natural impulses, as I have so often seen my son doing when he proudly shows his latest drawing, I become disheartened and tired.

I guess that the idea that "A man's praise in his own mouth stinks" stems from situations when someone did not celebrate fully, but sneakily showed how he had achieved something. This feels more like buying acceptance from the outside and is not a celebration. We may wonder how we can expect others to celebrate with us if we express ourselves this way.

When children celebrate, as they usually do, it's often done openly until they have learned something else, "Mom, Mom, I did it, look at what I did." That kind of celebration is usually easy to rejoice in, even when it is coming from adults.

One thing that helps me to be happy about having completed something and expressing appreciation to myself is to see myself as part of a chain of giving and receiving. Find out more about this under the heading "Your link in the chain of giving and receiving", on page 119.

Comparisons

Sometimes we compare ourselves with others in a way that gets in the way of appreciation. "Yes, he is good but not as good as..." Anyone who has discovered that comparisons reduce our ability to appreciate life and has therefore tried to quit comparing knows how difficult it is. It is often said that comparisons come "automatically" or "are ingrained" when the fact is that most of us have been trained to compare all your lives. Racing and competing to be better than others, has been with us since we were children.

On the notice board in my office hangs a tragicomic newspaper clipping. It depicts a mother who is dragging her two-year-old boy, wearing a vest with a race number on it, over the finish line. The subtitle explains – in a serious tone - that both the mother of this boy and other parents forced the children to finish the race. The children did not understand that the competition was about coming first, and would rather play with each other than to race to be first over the finishing line.

The kind of comparisons I'm referring to, are those based on "right and wrong" or "better and worse". Not about comparing wallpaper to see which wallpaper is darker than the other, or to compare choices of paths to find the shortest route to Tuscany. That kind of comparison, based on function, rather than morality is often helpful in making decisions. It is when we put a moral significance to the comparisons that it affects us in a negative way. Since "moral" comparisons so significantly affect our well-being, and I discovered that it was not so easy to stop comparing, I have devoted some energy to explore them.

Something I have benefited greatly from is the concept that all comparison reminds us about some important need. I became curious about my comparing and about how I could use them to better support my needs.

Four things to do when you catch yourself making comparisons:

- See them as reminders that you have had extensive practice in comparing.
- See them as reminders that you have gone astray and have temporarily forgotten what is important to you.
- See them as reminders that it's time to pause and find out what you feel, need and want.
- Remind yourself that behind every comparative thought you can find beautiful needs.

Appreciation Missing it's Target

- You never express what you appreciate about me.
- I thought I have often told you what I appreciate about you!
- Yes, but it feels more like a "pat on the head". I hear it as you are saying, "Oh, you're not so stupid after all! I'm surprised you have managed this so well, I did not know you were so talented."

Even if that was not what I was saying – this is what my friend had heard. Together we came to the conclusion that she was not hearing any longing about getting or learning anything from her. She realized that partly this was due to her image of me as her "teacher," "proficient" or even a "know-it -all." It made it difficult for her to hear my appreciation. She realized something that would make it was easier for her to receive my appreciation. It was if she had the experience of having done something that would help me meet my needs in a way I had never thought of before. Then she stopped hearing it as me "approving" of her.

It helped me to nuance my way of expressing myself. I learned to express that I had needs that hadn't been met, which I now could meet thanks to her. I could even use comparisons as a base to clarify this.

I changed - "When I hear you play the piano, I am so happy because I get so much inspiration," into:

"When I hear you play the piano, I am both happy and a little bit sad. Sad because I would like to be able to play myself and happy that it is still possible for me to hear music that inspires and nourishes *me*."

Chapter 4 – Happiness Tools

Happiness Comes, Happiness Goes

It is not the *intensity* of the pleasurable feelings that determines whether we experience happiness or not[1]. A powerful experience once a year (when we manage to buy something we long for) isn't what gives us a happy life. The answer to the quest for happiness is not to find an intense high of joy at a large adventure, of drugs, of having found the right partner, or by winning the lottery. If we yearn for a sustained sense of happiness other strategies are call for.

It is how often we experience happiness that determines whether we regard ourselves as happy. Finding happiness in small moments of pleasure and meaning in everyday life, in expressing kindness to others, to appreciate what we have, saying "Thank you" and meaning it, makes a real difference.

Later in this book you will find exercises on gratitude that are designed to give you a steady stream of joy and happiness in your everyday life. They are created to encourage you to create a lifestyle where you as often as possible give yourself a dose of happiness. I have often heard people ask what you do to be happy. During the past 20 years research has been done on what actually leads to greater happiness. The research results are growing all the time and we can use this information to make more aware choices. I'm inspired by an assumption from the philosophy of laughter yoga:

"*You do not laugh because you're happy, you're happy because you laugh.*"[2]

We talk about "finding happiness" or "being happy" as if happiness is a place or something we can "get" once and for all. To relate to happiness in this way is deceptive, because happiness has been shown to come from things we do every day or every week, rather

---

1 When I use the expression feeling happiness, I mean such emotions as joy, relief, curiosity, contentment, hopefulness, excitement or warmth.
22 One of the basic ideas of laughter yoga. http://svt.se/2.15856/1.338391/forbattra_din_hal med_skrattyoga? lid = puff_653506 & LPOS = extra_3 Retrieved 2 December 2010.

than being a static condition. Happiness mostly comes as a result, just as we will be happy by laughing. Happiness can be created and influenced to a high degree.

On the cover of her book "The How of Happiness", Sonja Lyubomirsky uses a circle diagram (symbolized by a round pie) to show what affects our happiness. The research she has compiled shows that about 50% of our happiness is based in our genetics (half the pie). That is, just as we can be born long or short, outward or inward, we have a baseline for how much happiness we experience.[3]

The remaining 50% of the pie is divided into two parts. Approximately 10 % of our happiness is calculated to be due to personal circumstances. For example, if you are married or single, rich or poor, unemployed, retired, in good health or not. A common way to try to create a happier life is to focus on trying to change theses circumstances. And even if it contributes to a slight increase in the degree of happiness it will be short-lived if it is not backed up with the remaining 40 % based on activities we regularly do that makes us happy.

If your most basic needs aren't met, it has a major impact on your happiness level. For those who live in impoverished and war-torn areas happiness is much more dependent on external circumstances than if you are a middle class person in Europe or USA.[4] I guess most people who are able to read this book belong to the group where people have most of their basic needs met and I also write from that perspective.

If we want to experience happiness and want to "invest smartly", we aim to change our own day-to-day behavior. Devoting all of our attention on changing our living conditions (the 10% of the pie) takes time and effort from the 40% where we can really do things that we can choose every day. This of course applies only to those of us, who already have our basic needs met, and are pleased with how our life looks like.

It can be a bigger challenge than you think to every day, or as

---

3 Lyubomirsky, Sonja (2008), The How of Happiness. A Scientific Approach to Getting the Life You Want. Penguin Putnam Inc.
4. One objection to research about happiness is that it is to a great extent made in the USA and Europe - in countries with high standard of living and relative political stability.

often as possible, choose to do things that make you happy. Maybe we are not entirely clear on what actually makes a difference, have habits that are hard to break, or have thoughts about not "deserving" to be happy.

When I began to write this section, I was genuinely worried that it was going to sound as if I am suggesting that we should not try to change structures that do not serve us. I hear people, who are inspired by the same sources as I am, concluding the best they can do is to "take care of oneself and not care about others." This approach scares me. I do not see happiness as a personal matter.

> **My choice of weekly happiness strategies:**
> Every day I try to do some kind of physical activity because it's one of my favorite happiness strategies. When I practice yoga it involves another of my favorite strategies - to meditate and invite spirituality in my life. Having decided to try to live a long and healthy life in order to get a lot of time with my child makes exercise extra important to me. So yoga and other exercises become "multi-strategies" that simultaneously meet many of my needs and support my happiness level.

Your genetic inheritance gives you a basic level but you can rise above that point by regularly choosing strategies for happiness that suits you. Research on so-called positive psychology and happiness shows that variety is important. Therefore try new ways to practice your happiness strategies. Also remember that "enduring" something that we know leads to a long-awaited goal, also has been shown to lead to happiness.

There is no predetermined path that leads to happiness forever and for everyone. Lyubomirsky has compiled 12 categories of strategies that according to research increase our level of happiness. To focus on gratitude has proven to be one of the ways to increase our experience of happiness.

You may think that it is easy to be thankful if you're happy, but the opposite is also true. Gratitude itself leads to greater happiness. Some of the answers to the question why gratitude is so valuable are that:

- Gratitude helps us to focus on experiencing and appreciate the good sides of life.

- Gratitude increases our self-esteem when it reminds us of the power we have to help others.

- Gratitude reduces our tendency to compare ourselves with others and instead increases our ability to listen with empathy to others.

- Gratitude reduces the "hedonic adaptation" which sometimes leads us to not seeing reality as it is and forgetting to be thankful for what we have.

- Gratitude helps us deal with stress and trauma. It makes us less anxious and depressed.

- Gratitude strengthens our social ties, gives inspiration to nourish new and existing relationships.

Happiness Creates Ripples on the Water

Shared joy - double joy!

I've often thought that happiness is nothing but a selfish luxury. When I learned that happiness might make our immune system stronger, I realized that an increased sense of happiness also can be seen as a "public benefit". Experiencing happiness increases our ability to deal with stress.

In addition, our creativity increases when we experience happiness and it also increases our ability to solve problems from a holistic perspective.[5]

To raise our level of happiness is valuable also for others around us because happy people co-operate better. It will affect both the mood

---

[5] Lyubomirsky, Sonja (2008), The How of Happiness. A Scientific Approach to Getting the Life You Want. Penguin Putnam Inc.

and the effectiveness in workplaces, families and other groups. When we feel happy, it's easier for us to lift our eyes and see other people and that makes it easier to create nurturing relationships. To be happy you need to choose to do what really makes you happy.

Happiness can thus be seen as a bi-product of doing things you enjoy - a receipt, rather than an end in itself. I no longer experience happiness as an end in itself. A goal might be, for example, writing a book. I love experiencing happiness that way.

Happiness is perishable and needs to be enjoyed every day. It cannot be stored or patented. It is available to all and grows as we nurture it. And in some mysterious way it also grows as we share it with others. One of the people who were in the "Gratitude Group" that during a year tested the 52 exercises in this book described her experience as follows:

I've learned that the more I feel thankful for what I have around me, the more I get to appreciate! It's like ripples on the water!
Carola

Twenty years of research suggests that what creates happy relationships is a balance between positive and negative expressions. In relationships that people experience as happy, about five positive things are expressed for each negative. It's easy to forget to express appreciation to friends and loved ones because we think they know we appreciate them. Taking it for granted gives the same result as when we forget to water our flowers.

Interestingly enough, research indicates that one factor that is characteristic to sustainable relationships is how to relate to each other in good times, not in hardship! If you express appreciation and celebrate together when things are going well for the other, it is easier to feel connected even when reality is tougher.

Not only does appreciation to our loved ones strengthen our relationships to them, but it also makes us feel good. For example one study shows that people who three times a day react with interest and enthusiasm to good news about friends, after only a week feel happier than at the beginning of the week. Appreciation has even been shown to lift depression.

Money and Happiness

Focusing on gratitude has given me joy, peace and reverence for the small things in life, not having as much "greed" as before. I settle for less and is more grateful for what I already have. I feel a kind of contentment over what I have and trust in that I get what I need.
Marianne

Some people say that "money will make you happy" and others say "it will not at all." Various researches show that both of these claims have a grain of truth in it. But there is no clockwork connection between those who have more money feeling happier than those who have less money, or vice versa.

The biggest misunderstanding might consist in what Daniel Gilbert so cleverly expresses, "we think that money will make us a lot happier for a long time, while in reality money makes us a little happier for a short time."

In most countries in the northern hemisphere, the economic growth has doubled, in some cases tripled, during the past decades, but it has not led to the same increase in the level of happiness. It is only when increased access to money helps people from severe poverty that it leads to greater happiness lasting over time. For those who already have material wealth, more money makes very little or no difference for the happiness level, Gilbert claims[6]. But for those who go from not having food for their children it can be understood that the level of happiness is significantly affected. I cannot even imagine that feeling of happiness and like many others I often take it for granted that I will have access to food to give my child. I agree with the psychologist Ruut Veenhoven who believes that a country that wants to increase people's happiness and well-being should focus less on measures to create economic growth and more on things that contribute to freedom, democracy, trust and public Safety.[7]

We are surrounded by the message (from movies, media, adver-

---

6. http://blog.ted.com/2006/09/happiness_exper.php 20100629
7. http://www2.eur.nl/fsw/research/veenhoven/

tising, music) that our need for meaning - a need that is important for us humans – will be met by getting possessions and being wealthy. When we do this misinterpretation of the need for meaning, it is easy to believe that more money automatically will make us happy. And we risk forfeiting being thankful for what we have. One explanation for why we do not get happier by possessing probably has to do with the hedonic adaptation, we get used to and adapt to the context we are in.

Then we resort to other means to experience happiness. And yes, you can replace a car, get a new job, divorce and find a new partner but often the more I do it, the more I need to do it to experience happiness. It is a real rat race where we have to run faster and faster to get the same kick. Studies show that the level of happiness in Europe and the United States has not increased since the mid-1900s, even though incomes have and this is one of the explanations.

Thus increased consumption does not lead to lasting happiness. Research about happiness shows that it is easier for people who feel happy to adapt if their income for any reason drops, and that they have an easier time letting go of consuming. We are not likely to consume more when we experience ourselves as happy, but rather the opposite.

Things that Happy People do[8]

1. Expressing gratitude
2. Cultivating optimism
3. Avoiding overthinking and social comparison
4. Practicing acts of kindness
5. Nurturing relationships
6. Developing strategies for coping
7. Learn to forgive and listen with empathy
8. Doing more activities that truly engage you (Flow)
9. Savoring life's joys
10. Committing to your goals
11. Practicing religion and spirituality
12. Taking care of your body

Your Happiness level

You cannot buy happiness or create it by any single action. Many of us believe in the myth that if we only can change our life circumstances, we will be happy. But we do not feel happy, at least not in the long run, because we have lots of money, when we get the "right" job or because we have found the "right" person to marry. Happiness comes from recurring actions that we are willing to repeat day after day, or at least every week of our lives.

Let's explore what you can do to create more happiness in your life. In the book "How of Happiness" Sonja Lyubomirsky describes

---

8. Twelve categories that research has shown leads to an increased level of happiness.

twelve research-based strategies in increasing happiness. There are things we can all do. Below you find a test I borrowed from her book.[9] This test is a way to try to find out how you actively create your own happiness.

In addition to these strategies, there are of course other things that contribute to our happiness, not necessarily less effective, but which have not yet been researched. Each of the 52 exercises that you will find further on in this book will in one way or the other be connected to these strategies for happiness. Use the test below either before starting the exercises or while you are doing them. Do this to strengthen your understanding of what works, or if you get stuck to get hints on how you can continue.

---

9. Lyubomirsky, Sonja (2008), The How of Happiness. A Scientific Approach to Getting the Life You Want. Penguin Putnam Inc.

Your Happiness Strategies - a Test and a Tool

This self-diagnostic test is an attempt to identify strategies that suit you best. Through a systematic, empirically based method it is determined which strategy for happiness (of the twelve) will benefit you the most. Use 15-30 minutes, preferably in a peaceful and quiet place to be able to really concentrate on completing it.

Instructions: Consider each of the following 12 happiness activities. Reflect on what it would be like to do it every week for an extended period of time. Then rate each activity by writing the appropriate number (1 to 7) in the blank space next to the terms NATURAL, ENJOY, VALUE, GUILTY, and SITUATION.
People do things for many different reasons. Rate why you might keep doing this activity in terms of each of the following reasons. Use this scale:
1=not at all 2, 3, 4 = somewhat 5, 6, 7= very much

NATURAL: I'll keep doing this activity because it will feel "natural" to me and I'll be able to stick with it.

ENJOY: I'll keep doing this activity because I will enjoy doing it; I'll find it to be interesting and challenging.

VALUE: I'll keep doing this activity because I will value and identify with doing it; I'll do it freely even when it's not enjoyable.

GUILTY: I'll keep doing this activity because I would feel ashamed, guilty, or anxious if I didn't do it; I'll force myself.

SITUATION: I'll keep doing this activity because somebody else will want me to or because my situation will force me to.

1) Expressing gratitude: Counting your blessings for what you have (either to a close other or privately, through contemplation or a journal) or conveying your gratitude and appreciation to one or more individuals whom you've never properly thanked.

Natural _____ Enjoy _____ Value _____ Guilty_____ Situation_____

2) Cultivating optimism:
Keeping a journal in which you imagine and write about the best possible future for yourself or practicing to look at the bright side of every situation.

Natural _____ Enjoy _____ Value _____ Guilty_____ Situation_____

3) Avoiding overthinking and social comparison: Using strategies (such as distraction) to cut down on how often you dwell on your problems and compare yourself with others.

Natural _____ Enjoy _____ Value _____ Guilty_____ Situation_____

4) Practicing acts of kindness: Doing good things for others, whether friends or strangers, either directly or anonymously, either spontaneously or planned.

Natural _____ Enjoy _____ Value _____ Guilty_____ Situation_____

5) Nurturing relationships: Picking a relationship in need of strengthening, and investing time and energy in healing, cultivating, affirming, and enjoying it.

Natural _____ Enjoy _____ Value _____ Guilty_____ Situation_____

6) Developing strategies for coping: Practicing ways to endure or surmount a recent stress, hardship, or trauma.

Natural _____ Enjoy _____ Value _____ Guilty_____ Situation_____

7) Learning to forgive: Keeping a journal or writing a letter in which you work on letting go of anger and resentment toward one or more individuals who have hurt or wronged you.

Natural _____ Enjoy _____ Value _____ Guilty_____ Situation_____

8) Doing more activities that truly engage you:
Increasing the number of experiences at home and work in which you "lose" yourself, which are challenging and absorbing (i.e., flow experiences).

Natural _____ Enjoy _____ Value _____ Guilty_____ Situation_____

9. Savoring life's joys: Paying close attention, taking delight, and replaying life's momentary pleasures and wonders, through thinking, writing, drawing, or sharing with another.

Natural _____ Enjoy _____ Value _____ Guilty_____ Situation_____

10. Committing to your goals: Picking one, two, or three significant goals that are meaningful to you and devoting time and effort to pursuing them.

Natural _____ Enjoy _____ Value _____ Guilty_____ Situation_____

11. Practicing religion and spirituality: Becoming more involved in your church, temple, or mosque or reading and pondering spiritually themed books.

Natural _____ Enjoy _____ Value _____ Guilty_____ Situation_____

12. Taking care of your body: Engaging in physical activity, meditating, and smiling and laughing.
Natural _____ Enjoy _____ Value _____ Guilty_____ Situation_____

How to calculate your best "fit" score and determine you set of best-fitting activites.

STEP 1: For each of the 12 activities, subtract the average of the GUILTY and SITUATION rating from the average of the NATURAL, ENJOY, and VALUE ratings.
In other words, for each of the 12 activities:
FIT SCORE = (NATURAL + ENJOY + VALUE)/ 3 - (GUILTY + SITUATION)/2

Step 2: Write down the four activities with the highest FIT SCORES.

1)

2)

3)

4)

Motivation

Some wonder why motivation seems to play such a central role in the test. Is it not most important *what* we do, rather than *why* we do it? The answer is quite simple. When something is perceived as natural, it is easier to implement it. If we feel happy when we do or feel pride that we act in accordance with our values, the strategy will be even easier to do. We need to feel inspired and are often encouraged by experiencing the excitement of being challenged. If we experience an outer or inner coercion to do something, it can motivate us, but only for a short time or as long as the coercion remains. Doing something motivated by coercion can suck the joy even out of the most enjoyable things.

Guilt and shame gives a kind of reverse motivation because we tend to be willing to do a lot to avoid feeling these feelings.[10]

If we do something driven by guilt the result itself is spoiled because we do not feel joy when we do it. The same applies when we do something out of fear of losing a reward or because we otherwise will be punished. It's not just what we do that matters, but what drives us to do so.

---

10 Larsson, Liv (2010), Anger, guilt and shame, Reclaiming Power and Choice. Friare Liv. Here you can read more on how anger and guilt not only affects our motivation but our whole inner landscape.

Chapter 5 - Welcome to the Happiness Gym

One Year of Gratitude

It is said that after a number of slalom victories, Swedish skier Ingemar Stenmark is supposed to have responded thus after being told by a journalist, *"How lucky you are – you've won again!"*... Ingemar, in his quiet way said, *"Yes, isn't it strange that the more I practice, the luckier I get ..."* [1]

Believe it or not our ability to experience gratitude can be trained. You can use the following 52 exercises in gratitude, one per week during a year to develop your gratitude muscles. You will already notice the results of how the exercises affect your level of happiness after a few weeks.

Some of the exercises I suggest that you do every day during the week, others just once. A few of them last over several weeks with some additions every week. You can start doing the exercises any time during the year. I suggest that you start with the exercise for week 1 to get the most out of the exercises, as they sometimes build on each other. You can, of course, continue longer than a week with an exercise if it is fruitful for you, and skip an exercise that doesn't fit you. Some exercises are repeated a few times to support you in going deeper. Remember that it is not the *amount* of exercise that will raise your happiness level, it's *how* you are doing them that gives results.

These exercises are suggestions on how to cultivate and nourish a feeling of gratitude and give inspiration to ways of expressing appreciation to yourself and others. They are also practical tools that have great potential in helping you experience more happiness in your life.

Be sure to find your own way to invite more gratitude in your life, as what gives us happiness is individual. Our ability to adapt often plays a trick on us, so be aware if you start doing the exercises routinely. If you feel that you cannot reach the core of gratitude even if you have done an exercise for some time, it may be an exercise that simply does not suit you. However, it is more likely that it would be valuable to you if you did a version of it. Maybe you put pressure on yourself to "do it right" and then the joy easily disappears. Experiment with doing the exercises less often or with a different attitude.

Research has shown that some people get the most out of writing a gratitude journal once a day, while others every other day, and still others as infrequently as once a week. Some people experience deeper gratitude in connection with others, than in focusing on gratitude alone such as in writing a gratitude journal. If you get more out of doing exercises together with someone than alone, I recommend that you do the exercises in the book that include expressing and receiving appreciation to and from someone else.

Other people get more out of taking a moment of solitary reflection and focusing on, for example, journaling. For them it might be draining to try to include others in their gratitude practice, at least in the beginning.

Another way to get in touch with gratitude, rather than just "doing an exercise" is to be silent for a few seconds and quietly repeat the word "thanks" a few times. This little word often makes me more ready to open up for gratitude.

I suggest that you ask yourself before you do an exercise if you want to do it and aren't doing it because you should. Reminding yourself that you always have a choice is a way to prepare yourself for more gratitude. It can also help you to learn more about what happiness strategies support you the most.

When I focus on connecting my feeling of gratitude to the needs that are met, I often experience that the feelings of gratitude deepened. They become deeper than if I just think about what I'm grateful for. Before you give up an exercise because you do not get as much out of it as you'd like, ask yourself whether you have taken the time to connect to the needs behind the gratitude you are exploring. Especially in the exercises where focusing on needs has been included, it is valuable to take plenty of time to stop not only to think about which need is met but to be affected by the essence of it.

By doing the test about strategies for happiness on page 76 you might have realized what happiness strategies suit you best. Choosing exercises that match them can provide direct feedback and create motivation to continue with the exercises that may seem unfamiliar or uncomfortable, or that you judge as "airy- fairy".

To succeed in inviting more gratitude support from others is invaluable. When the exercises were "tested", it was clear that it was a great support to the participants to share what they had learned with others. They got ideas about what they could do if they got stuck, and exchanged ideas on variations of exercises. A suggestion on how to proceed with your gratitude year is to gather a group (friends, colleagues, family members) who are interested in exploring gratitude together. Maybe you meet physically, via cyberspace, or in any other form such as by telephone. If you do not manage to gather a group of people together, maybe you can get a "happiness friend". Also tell friends and family what you intend to do. We succeed in changing our habits to a much greater extent when we tell others about our plans, than when we keep them to ourselves.

To get the maximum yield from these exercises, it is valuable that you decide to do them regularly. Feel free to set goals for how long you want do a certain exercise, and periodically stop and evaluate how it goes.

Remember that happiness is not something we have or can find; it's something we create and is created by the way we live every day. So get ready for some tools to make gratitude part of your daily lifestyle.

Preparations

- Take a moment to ask yourself what is motivating you before you start doing the exercises. What are you longing to have more of in your life that you hope these exercise will contribute to?

- Make a "gratitude journal" in which you write down appreciation, insights and more.

- Fill in the happiness strategies test on page 76 to get clarity around what strategies fit you in order to know how to stay motivated.

- Fill in the Oxford happiness Survey on page 169. Keep the answers for a month, or at least until you do the survey again. Once you have done the survey a second time, compare your numbers with the first round and so on. Please mark the date in your calendar to remember to do this once a month for 6 - 12 months.

Instructions

1. The book contains a program for 52 weeks, but you can do the exercises less often, more often, or for longer if it supports you more.

2. Some of the exercises are based on a previous one so make sure to read the exercise beforehand or do them in chronological order.

3. Remember most importantly to let each exercise affect you, not to do as many as possible.

4. If there is any exercise that contributes to you more, feel free to continue with it as long as you want. Also remember that some of them come back, sometimes as they are and sometimes with an addition or in a variant form.

5. If you cannot find the motivation to do any exercise, go back to an exercise you have experienced as more meaningful or fun.

6. If you lose motivation to do a particular exercise, go back to the happiness strategies test to get clues about what exercises you can choose instead. Also read the section "If the fire of motivation fades away" on page 160.

7. If you live without a predictable daily schedule, instead of doing the exercises every day, you can make sure to set aside a specific time once a week or in some other way that fits.

8. Reflect regularly about whether you are doing the exercises for a reason that isn't nourishing you. For example if you do them out of guilt, shame, in the hope of reward or fear of punishment.

9. If you want to grow, try to do an exercise, even if you think it's unclear, weird, uncomfortable or airy-fairy.

52 Exercises to Build Gratitude Muscles

Week 1

Gratitude Diary

Invite yourself, preferably somewhere between three to seven times during this week, to make a list of things you appreciate. There may be three points or more for every time you write. Consider whether it suits you best to do this in the morning, in the evening before going to sleep, or at some other specific time during the day. Write without stopping for 5 - 10 minutes. This is a basic exercise to stimulate gratitude that you can always go back to if any of the other exercises do not suit you.

Then read through the list and notice how it feels when you remind yourself of what you appreciate and are grateful for. Save the list to be able to use it during the following week and throughout the year in various exercises. If you like, write a summary of what you discovered at the end of the week.

Remember! Fill in the Oxford overview of happiness on page 87 before you start writing the gratitude journal. This will provide you with feedback in the future, so that you can measure your changes over time.

Variation: I want to demonstrate how you can vary this first exercise. I want to do this because the exercises do not have the desired effect if you are experiencing (internal or external) demands on performing them the "right way". For example, you can vary the exercise by writing in the gratitude journal over several weeks. Write in it one to seven times a week deepening on what attracts you. Take time for reflection. It can be gratitude to yourself, gratitude for what someone else has done, for something or someone close to you, or for something that has happened earlier in your life.

Write at least once a week and reflect on if you think it would help you to write more often. Do not write so often that you start to feel resistance or it becomes a routine. Write in a way that helots you feel joy and connects you to celebration. You might also get support in just starting the journaling with I am grateful for ... or I am celebrating ...

If you do not enjoy writing, you can instead take the time to simply think about the things you are grateful for. Maybe focus on something you normally take for granted or something you appreciate every time you think about it. For some people it might be helpful to list 5 things that you are grateful for to give you more structure.

I noticed that I had difficulties in feeling appreciation some mornings. It was when I started to have my gratitude journal nearby - to be able to write a few words there and then that I felt the exercise had an effect on me.
Johan

It makes a difference on my degree of appreciation if I am specific. I easily feel gratitude when I think of water. But the gratitude deepens when I connect to "special waters", for example, the lapping water at the pier at the canoe club.
Birgitta

Might work especially well if you have a high score on happiness strategies:
1. (Expressing gratitude)
2. (Cultivating optimism)
9. (Enjoying the pleasures of life)

Week 2

Enjoying Gratitude

Use the list from last week, and eventually add something new and fresh. Every day you select one to three of the items on the list, which you then focus on at that moment. Notice how you feel when you focus on them. When the feeling is clear, ask yourself what needs are met in relation to what you are grateful for. Use the list of needs at the end of the book as support in finding needs (page 89). Consider whether it suits you best to do this in the morning, in the evening before going to sleep, or at some other point during the day. Maybe you want to put up the list of things you are grateful for somewhere where you can read it from time to time over the next few weeks. Write down what you experienced or learned at the end of the week.

I discovered that I'm trying to hold on to the idea that some things still mean something special to me. I noticed that it made a big difference when I let go of that and took the time to connect to the actual needs that were met during the day in order to get a deeper connection and a stronger sense of gratitude.
    Johan

This is a great start of the day.
    Birgitta

> Might work especially well if you have a high score on happiness strategies:
> 2. (Cultivating optimism)
> 6. (Learning to endure)
> 9. (Enjoying life)

Week 3

Appreciating Somebody Else

Use a few moments each day during this week to reflect on what a specific person in your neighborhood has done that you appreciate. Connect to what need of yours the other person's actions met. Take your time and really allow yourself to be affected by the action and the met needs. Perhaps by taking a deep breath and connecting with how it feels in the area of your heart.

Reflect on whether it suits you best to do this in the morning, in the evening before going to sleep, or some other time during the day. Perhaps it suits you better to write appreciation on one or two occasions during the week instead of every day. Formulate the appreciation, as you would like to present it to the person concerned. Save what you write for next week.

Through this exercise, I realized how I could appreciate someone and still have difficulties in finding words to express it. Looking for and finding more words deepened the appreciation.
Elisabeth

Might work especially well if you have a high score on happiness strategies:
2. (Cultivating optimism)
4. (Practicing acts of kindness)
5. (Nurturing relationships)
7. (Learning to forgive and to listen with empathy)

Week 4

Expressing Your Appreciation

Express one appreciation for every day during this week to someone around you. You can choose from what you wrote last week or express something else. Feel free to do it on several occasions and to several people and reflect on how it affects you.

Please connect with the person and express what you have seen the person do or heard him or her say, what you feel when you think about it, and what needs were met by it.

Maybe you also want to ask how the recipient feels hearing the appreciation. It may not be possible to express appreciation directly in all situations; in that case you can instead call or write a letter. End the week with writing a summary of what you discovered.

I get so excited when I express appreciation - especially when I make it a conscious choice. I love to tell someone that what he or she has done or said touched me. I do not know if it's them or me who gets the most out of it really.
Linda

Might work especially well if you have a high score on happiness strategies:
2. (Cultivating optimism)
4. (Practicing acts of kindness)
5. (Caring relationships)
7. (Learning to forgive and to listen with empathy)

Week 5

Appreciating Yourself

Take a few moments three times or more during this week, to express appreciation to yourself. Write down when you've done something you really appreciate. It can be something you've done the last day or something you did long ago, but that you recall today. Big or small does not matter.

Then connect to the needs that were met by what you did. Allow yourself to experience the feeling stimulated by thinking of this appreciation. Consider whether it suits you best to do this in the morning, in the evening before going to sleep, or at any other time during the day.

Write a summary of your reflections at the end of the week. Is there a difference between expressing appreciation to another person and to yourself? What then is the difference? What similarities are there?

If you think this seems like a challenge, read the paragraph entitled "A man's praise in his own mouth stinks".

When did I last take a pause to say thank you to myself? The question hurts me, like a sharp knife. How often do I stop and marvel at all I manage to do, all I'm actually able or can do? Not often because I am in such a damned hurry to get to the next thing. Performing has become so central. It is so nice to stop and just be for once.
Elisabeth

Might work especially well if you have a high score on happiness strategies:
3. (Avoiding comparisons)
6. (Developing strategies for coping)
9. (Enjoying life)

2nd Happiness Survey

Fill in the Oxford Happiness Survey on page 169 and save it in a place where you can easily find it in four weeks. When you have completed the survey, compare your numbers with the first round if you did it before you started.

I suggest that you mark the date on your calendar to remind you to do this once a month for 6 - 12 months. It is a great opportunity to get helpful feedback.

Week 6

Gratitude Diary

This week we go back to the gratitude journal we started in week 1. (Please read that text again.) Take it slowly and allow yourself to enjoy the gratitude that is stimulated. Continue to write down more of what you are grateful for. Maybe it leads to something that may resemble poems like the one below.

I live in gratitude.
I am grateful that I exist in this life.
I am grateful for the qualities and abilities that I have and for having been born as the person I am.
I am grateful for the family I have and the friends I've met through life.
I am grateful to everyone who has come my way, and thus taught me something about life.
I am grateful that I have had the opportunity to develop my own special potential in life.
I am grateful for all the experiences I have had and still receive more of every day.
I am grateful for my ability to enjoy life and the beauty available on this planet.
I am grateful that I can laugh and rejoice with my surroundings.
I am grateful for my dreams as they bring me pleasure, and for the love I feel towards myself, my loved ones, and in moments of total gratitude also to the whole, the universe.
I am grateful for the sense of purpose I experience and the guidance I receive from one day to another that leads me towards new exciting experiences.[1]

---

1 www.kreativinsikt.se 26 juni 2010.

I have written a gratitude journal a few times, but never found the energy to keep on doing it. However, I have found another way that works great for me. In the evenings when I go to bed I reflect on what I'm grateful for. Feels like talking to God!
Carola

I discovered that during difficult days I had more things I experienced gratitude for. When I was faced with challenges, I often needed to ask for support and could clearly see how my life is interconnected with other people and how they are willing to support me when I need it.

Linda

> Might work especially well if you have a high score on happiness strategies:
> 2. (Cultivating optimism)
> 3. (Avoiding comparisons)
> 9. (Enjoying life)

Week 7

Doing Nothing

So many people are afraid of silence.
If they only for a moment dared to listen, they would discover that silence is really not silence at all.
They would discover that silence is an underground water song, a deep river speaking the truth in a never ending stream.

They would have discovered that the silence surrounding all life with tender hands, watering it with quite deep thoughts, making it grow.
They would discover that silence is the eternal mother watching over the rock crib of life.
Maria Vine

For at least five minutes each day during this week, do nothing. I suggest that you start by reading the text about Sabbath in Chapter 2. When you are doing physical training the same principle applies as when you are farming, only after resting can you reap what you have sown. The same is true with this training program.

Set an alarm so you can drop focus on time. Please write a reflective summary at the end of the week in which you notice if something has happened that affects your sense of gratitude.

Several times during this week I thought that five minutes is a long time. To avoid thinking about the time I set the alarm (soft tone) on my mobile, it made it easier to relax completely. After only a minute of silence, I felt done. To continue being still was at first a challenge, but in the end of the week it turned into a pleasure.
Katarina

Might work especially well if you have a high score on happiness strategies:
6. (Developing strategies for coping)
8. (Flow)
9. (Enjoying life)
11. (Practicing religion and spirituality)
12. (Meditation and taking care of the body)

Week 8

Receiving Appreciation

Imagine you are going to ask someone that you know if there is something you have done that he or she appreciates. What do you feel when you think of asking for it? What needs are these feelings telling you about?

Take a moment on one or more occasions during this week to write down what you would like someone to express appreciation to you about. What appreciation would you like to hear from someone else? Ask yourself what it is that makes you want this particular appreciation? If you imagine that someone expresses this appreciation - what need of yours would be met. What do you feel when you get in touch with these needs?

A variation and deepening of this exercise is to read the appreciation you have written out loud to yourself and really take time to let it sink in and affect you.

There is a small "Jante" on my shoulder shouting "you are not worth this", "why should you have it, think of how many people never get to experience this..." Thoughts of "deserve" arise as fast as an express train. I am really looking forward to confronting this, as I need to hear if I do some things that matter to people.
Lennart

Sometimes I mourn having forgotten to express something I appreciate and then it's nice when someone asks me for appreciation. I usually remind myself of the value this request has for me, when I feel reluctant to ask others if they want to hear something that I am grateful for.
Maria

Might work especially well if you have a high score on happiness strategies:
3. (Avoiding comparisons)
5. (Cherishing relationships)
6. (Developing strategies for coping)
9. (Enjoying life)

Week 9

Asking for Appreciation

Request to hear from one or more persons something they appreciate about you. Perhaps be particular and check if they are grateful for some of the things that you wrote down last week. Ideally ask a few different people. Maybe settle for one per day to have time to absorb the answers.

Ask them to clarify themselves if it is not clear to you what you have done or said that they appreciate. Guess what needs were met or ask them which of their needs were met. Take a moment to notice how it feels for you to hear the answer.

To ask about the needs that have been met by something we have done can help us to get away from the thought that the other is "trying to get something from us" with their appreciation.

Maybe you want to remind yourself that by your question you make it possible for others to experience that wonderful feeling you get by expressing appreciation. Here are some suggestions on how you can ask if it feels challenging:

At work with a colleague:
I wonder if today or recently I've done something that you like?

If the person looks puzzled, you may want to add:
"I ask because I want to learn about how and if I contribute to others. I'd like to understand if what I do matters to you? Is this clearer?

Or
"Right now, I am not sure about what and if I am adding something to this project by my working on it. Can you think of anything I have said or done that has somehow contributed to you or the project?"

With your friends or someone close to you, you might ask:
"Would you tell me whether I have enriched your life in any way?"

Or:

"Would you tell me if I have somehow helped you today or on some other day?"

If they say something we recognize, we can also guess how it has enriched the person. That is trying to connect with the person's feelings and needs.

If you want to ask a small child, you can try something like: *"Dad is curious, has Dad done something you like today? Be prepared to be surprised by the answers!"*

During the week, I noticed that several people were happy that I asked and it was not quite what I expected. Although I myself usually feel happy when someone asks me!
Elisabeth

I sometimes mourn that I have forgotten to express something I appreciate - I realize that it's really nice to be asked.
Marianne

I am glad to be reminded that I can ask for this. Sure, it was scary at first but it is incredibly valuable.
Mary

Might work especially well if you have a high score on happiness strategies:
3. (Avoiding comparisons)
5. (Cherishing relationships)
6. (Learning to endure)

Week 10

Thanking the Day!

Who feeds the birds
who rises the sun
Who makes the moon shine
Why do you worry so?
Do you give the sunset a standing ovation
For once again, performing a miracle right before your eyes
And do you anoint the river with blessings for flowing year after year?

This exercise you can do in the evening, perhaps just before you fall asleep. Focus on what you are grateful for this day. Maybe you want to say it out loud or just to think about it. If it makes it easier for you to focus, you can write down things that happened during the day that you appreciate and what caused it to happen. For some it is easier to decide how many things to write down, preferably three to five.

After this, take a moment to enjoy your list. Then connect these events to the needs they met, because it tends to make it easier to enjoy them.

Maybe you prefer to do this exercise with your children or someone in your family and together share your gratitude for the day. Do this every day during this week, or as often as it is fun and meaningful.

One effect of doing this exercise has been that I have been more aware of both getting appreciation and giving appreciation than I normally am. And I have enjoyed it.
Maria

Oh how much there is to experience gratitude for. I'm blown away!
Linda

Might work especially well if you have a high score on happiness strategies:
1. (Expressing gratitude)
2. (Cultivating optimism)
9. (Enjoying life)
11. (Practicing religion and spirituality)

Week 11

Express Appreciation to Someone Else

Express appreciation to others around you during this week. Get in touch with which of your needs that person's actions met. Take your time to really allow yourself to be affected by the actions and the met needs. One way is by taking a deep breath and another way is by connecting to the area around your heart. Try to do it on several occasions and with several people, and note how it affects you. Use a moment as often as you choose during this week to reflect on what appreciations you would like to express.

Start by asking the person if he or she wants to hear your appreciation and express why you want to share it. After that express what you have seen or heard him do or say, what needs were met by it, and what you felt when you connected with the met need.

Expressing my gratitude gives me some kind of confidence that I will have more to be thankful for. It might have to do with the fact that when you focus on gratitude then you become more grateful. It becomes a sort of self-fulfilling prophecy!
Carola

   Might work especially well if you have a high score on happiness strategies:
   1. (Expressing gratitude)
   4. (Practicing acts of kindness)
   5. (Caring for relationships)

3rd Happiness Survey

Fill in the Oxford Happiness Survey on page 169 and save it in a place where you can easily find it in four weeks. When you have completed the survey, compare your numbers with the first round if you did it before you started.

I suggest that you mark the date on your calendar to remind you to do this once a month for 6 - 12 months. It is a great opportunity to get feedback.

Week 12

Appreciating Yourself

Use a short moment, at least three times during this week, to express appreciation to yourself.

Write down what you did that you appreciate. It can be something you've done in the last day or something that you did long ago. Big or small does not matter. Then connect to the needs that were met by what you did. Also connect to what feelings it stimulates to think of this appreciation and to connect with the met needs. Reflect on whether you perceive a difference between expressing appreciation to yourself and giving it to someone else.

Consider whether it suits you best to do it in the morning, in the evening before going to sleep, or at some other time.

When I suddenly find a small piece of the puzzle and see something that I have not seen before, it feels so nice and warm inside. I am filled with some sort of wonder and joy that just flows. I dream of making a difference in the world and even if I do less than I dream of, I receive more clarity about what I actually do to live that dream. Living the way I preach!
Linda

> Might work especially well if you have a high score on happiness strategies:
> 2. (Cultivating optimism)
> 3. (Avoiding comparisons)
> 9. (Enjoying life)

Week 13

Quarterly Evaluation

This week is a time to reflect, take time to read through your gratitude journal, notes, and other things you've written so far, and to enjoy what you have achieved. If this does not suit you, or if it doesn't feel meaningful, you can repeat any of the previous exercises (see more on that in week 14) or do the exercise for week 15.

Take the time to rejoice and celebrate what you have done so far to experience more happiness and gratitude in your life. Reflect on what it has given you to focus on gratitude and clarify to yourself how you want to precede. Perhaps some of the questions below can be helpful.

1. Do you have one or more favorite exercise?

2. Is there any exercise you feel hesitant about or did not get anything out of? What can you learn from it, for example about what happiness strategies suit you the best?

3. What has helped you to continue doing the exercises?

4. What has made it challenging to keep doing them? Do you see any pattern in this?

> Might work especially well if you have a high score on happiness strategies:
> 2. (Cultivating optimism)
> 9. (Savoring life's joys).
> 10. (Committing to your goals).

Week 14

Choose what Works for You

My hope is that last week's reflective evaluation gave you some clues as to what type of exercises give you the most satisfaction and learning, so that it is easy to see which of the exercises you want to do again.

Some of the exercises that I've heard people appreciate doing regularly are: expressing appreciation to oneself or to others, "doing nothing" and writing in the gratitude journal. Maybe you want to write in the gratitude journal focusing on what you are grateful for when others succeed in something, in accordance with the concept Mudita. See page 14.

As soon as I mix up a "should" with the appreciation exercises, I lose the joy. Therefore I usually sit in silence for a while before I decide what I want to choose to do.
   Mats

Might work especially well if you have a high score on happiness strategies:
2. (Cultivating optimism)
8. (Flow)
9. (Enjoying life)
10. (Setting goals)

Week 15

Thanking Your Food!

Begin one or more of your meals by giving thanks for the food. This is a tradition in many cultures and families but has been lost by many. You can do this in a simple way by simply thinking or saying "thank you". You can take a moment to look at your food and remind yourself of the special honor of having it on your plate, or just saying thank you when your plate is empty and your stomach is full.

Perhaps it suits you better to give thanks for the food in a more ceremonial manner. You can remind yourself that the food is a gift from the earth, the air, and a variety of organisms, the animal world and from other people who in different ways have contributed to the food now being on your plate. You can also do this by some kind of prayer.

I say thanks! There is food for me. I say thanks for letting me get the strength and energy to live my life with the help of this food. Previously, I regarded saying grace as an empty gesture. I like the "prayer" you suggested, but chose to do my thanks more informally to prevent the moment from developing into an empty ritual. I connect with my gratefulness for the food I receive and pay reverence to all that preceded it's ending up on my plate. Sometimes I am moved to tears. Pausing to connect with wonders before eating has made me enjoy the food more, to really taste it and I notice that I have even started to chew more slowly.
   Birgitta

I tried all week. It did not work at all. I simply forgot it every time I was to eat. I tried to remind myself several times, but when I sat down to eat, I never remembered. I thought that perhaps I take it for granted that I have food, so it just does not come naturally to even say an internal "thanks for the food." I have simply had to say thanks for the food whenever I have remembered to do it.
Elisabeth

Might work especially well if you have a high score on happiness strategies:
1. (Expressing gratitude)
9. (Enjoying life)
12. (Meditation and taking care of the body)

Week 16

Gratitude Over Met Needs

Select one or more occasions this week when you can focus on one or two of the following needs. (You can, of course, choose some completely different needs than those listed below). Maybe you want to do this immediately after waking up and thereby "carry it with you" throughout the day. Or, you might want to do it in the evening before going to sleep in order to bring it into your dreams. Focus on how it feels to remember those moments when that need is met.

If a week seems too short for this exercise, then you can choose to do it over a longer time, perhaps using a week per need for as long as it feels right.

Think about and write down a situation where this need has been satisfied, maybe today, recently or long ago. You can choose different needs each day if you want to broaden your exploration. You can also choose to focus on one need throughout the week if you want to deepen your connection to that particular need and what place it has in your life.

Meaning	Love
Empathy	Freedom
Community	Mutuality
Hope	To be seen
Rest	Integrity

I've managed this by choosing a need for the following day already in the evening before I go to sleep. It has worked well for me!
Katarina

Might work especially well if you have a high score on happiness strategies:
1. (Expressing gratitude)
2. (Cultivating optimism)
9. (Enjoying life)
11. (Practicing religion and spirituality)

4th Happiness Survey

Fill in the Oxford Happiness Survey on page 169 and save it in a place where you can easily find it in four weeks. When you have completed the survey, compare your numbers with the first round if you did it before you started.

I suggest that you mark the date on your calendar to remind you to do this once a month for 6 - 12 months. It is a great opportunity to get feedback.

Week 17

Connecting Needs to Gratitude

Choose one of the needs you have explored during the previous week. It may be the need that affected you the most or the least. Maybe you connected to a need you want to learn more about or explore more deeply. During this week make a list on how you can celebrate this need. How can you meet it in as many ways as possible?

How can you let others know about it, how they have helped you get this need met, and specifically what it was that they did? Perhaps you will be reminded of previous situations where the need was also met and situations where you have not expressed appreciation to someone for helping you with it - maybe there is still a possibility to do this?

I notice I easily use many words when I try to express appreciation to someone and meanwhile I notice that I am often not as clear about which needs have been met. I probably express enough emotion with body language, and less frequently with words. Therefore this was a great help in starting to do it also in words.
Elisabeth

Might work especially well if you have a high score on happiness strategies:
2. (Cultivating optimism)
8. (Flow)
9. (Enjoying life)
11. (Practicing religion and spirituality)
12. (Meditation)

Week 18

Who Wants Appreciation?

Step 1: Ask at least three people this week if they would like to hear appreciation from you more often, or if they want to hear appreciation from you right now. Select any number of people. You can focus on all in one day or someone new every day during the week. It could be someone in your family, friends or colleagues, or anyone you think would like to hear your appreciation. Try different ways to ask and if you get a no, consider whether you can make your question more inviting.

(If you feel strong resistance to asking, begin to formulate appreciation for others and after having done so, ask yourself again if you want to express it aloud.)

Step 2: Tell the person what you have seen them do or heard him or her say, what you feel when you think about it, and what needs of yours were met by it.

Maybe you also want to ask the person how it is for him or her to hear the appreciation. It may not be possible to express the appreciation to the person directly. In that case you might call or write instead, but make sure that you are connected with whether or not the other person wants to hear the appreciation before you express it.

Note what happens inside of you before, during, and after you express the appreciation. You will find some of the questions that those who tried this exercise before have written below. They both agonized and had fun when they were experimenting with a few different ways:

"Is there anything you do for me that you would like me to express my appreciation about more clearly?"

"You do a lot of things that I never thank you for; is there anything you would like to hear a thank you for that I have missed?"

"Is there anything you do that you would really like me to express my appreciation for?"

"I know you have said that you understand through my smiles and laughter that I appreciate what you do. Can you think of any situation where you would want me to express my thanks also in words?"

"I'm worried that I have missed out on expressing appreciation to you many times. Is that so?"

"Would you like me to tell you why I value our relationship so much?"

"I would like to tell you what I like about you. Do you want to hear what I have to say?"

"I have often thought that I would like to thank you and tell you what it is that makes me enjoy being with you so much. Is it okay if I tell you now?"

"I wonder if you know that I appreciate you and what you do, and if there is anything you would like to hear that I appreciate about you?"

"I am worried that I have not made it clear to you that I appreciate you, is this clear to you? Do you want to hear more about it?"

"I wonder if there is something you long to hear that I value you for?"

>Might work especially well if you have a high score on happiness strategies:
>3. (Avoiding overthinking and social comparison.)
>4. (Practicing acts of kindness)
>5. (Nurturing relationships)
>7. (Learning to forgive and to listen with empathy)

Week 19

Appreciating Your Body

Take a few moments each day during this week, or as many time as it feels good, to appreciate your body. You can sit, stand, lie or walk when you do this exercise. Start to feel how your body feels right now. Focus for a moment on the places that feel comfortable. Then connect with your heart. It is beating and beating, minute after minute, hour after hour, day after day, and year after year. Ask yourself if you appreciate the job that your heart does in keeping you alive?

Then connect with another organ and what that organ does. Is there something you appreciate about this? Is there anything else you want to appreciate your body for?

Avoid "forcing" appreciation by thinking that you "should" be grateful. Instead note if you are experiencing gratitude even in a small way. Summarize what you have learned at the end of the week.

It is not always important for me to put appreciation into words. It's more about the connection with my body and how I hold myself.
Birgitta

> Might work especially well if you have a high score on happiness strategies:
> 9. (Savoring life's joys:)
> 11. (Practicing religion and spirituality)
> 12. (Meditation and Taking care of your body)

Week 20

Emotions as Clues to Gratitude

Feelings are important. They tell us what we need and how important it is for us to try to meet those needs. Therefore, this week we will explore how our feelings can give us clues about gratitude experiences we might have missed fully enjoying.

Step 1: Read through the list of feelings below. These are feelings we experience when our needs are met. Select a feeling and remind yourself of any time when you felt this, perhaps recently. Be as specific as you can with what happened, so that you can also connect it to the needs that were met.

Step 2: Remind yourself of a time you felt that feeling when someone else expressed appreciation to you. What needs were met for you and for the other person?

Step 3: Remind yourself of a time you felt that feeling when you expressed appreciation to someone else. Which needs were met for both you and the other person?

Do this exercise at least once this week and more if you feel like it. Take the time that you need to really connect with the feeling and the need to let it sink in. Feel the result in expressing gratitude to yourself or to others.

> **Feelings we might experience when our needs are met:**
>
> Gratitude, joy, satisfaction, hopefulness, inspiration, peace, faith, relief, relaxation, energy, fascination, excitement, contentment, optimism, alertness, elation, calmness.

For me, all the positive feelings are closely connected with gratitude. Every time I really take in and stay with a positive emotion, I also fill up with gratitude.
Birgitta

Might work especially well if you have a high score on happiness strategies:
1. (Expressing gratitude)
2. (Cultivating optimism)
9. (Savoring life's joys).

Week 21

Expressing Appreciation

Express one appreciation to someone every day of this week or express many appreciations to several people in a single day if it suits you better.

Do it on several occasions and express gratitude to several people and notice how it affects you. Notice the similarities and the differences from one person to another. Connect with each person and tell them what you have heard him or her do or say, what you feel and what needs were met by their action.

Maybe you also want to ask the person how it is for him or her to hear your appreciation. It may not be possible at all times to express this to them directly. In such cases you can call or write instead. Write a summary of what you have learned at the end of the week.

I wrote a letter to a person where I expressed how much I appreciated our relationship. I described what she had done that I was grateful for and what needs of mine were met. It has really deepened our connection. She also expressed that she was glad to hear from me because it confirmed to her that we are connected.
Marianne

Might work especially well if you have a high score on happiness strategies:
4. (Practicing acts of kindness).
5. (Nurturing relationships).
7. (Learn to forgive and listen with empathy).

Week 22

Your Link in the Chain of Giving and Receiving

We are now going back to one of the original exercises, but with a variation. Take a few moments of each day, or at least once this week, to express appreciation to yourself in writing.

Write down something you've done that you really appreciate. It can be something you've done in the last day or something that you did long ago. Then connect with the needs that were met by what you did and what you feel now when you connect with those needs.

When you feel connected to the met needs, ask yourself: "What have I been given, that has made it possible for me to do what I am grateful for?" Let the response touch and nurture you if you can.

When we feel that we are part of a context, a chain of people and events in which we give and receive, it is often easier to feel gratitude. When we take a pause and think about how we are all interconnected, it is easier to experience wonder and appreciate what we have received. Everything - from the food on my plate to the clothes I wear - is there because I'm part of this "chain". Gratitude usually heightens the experience of being part of a context.

Thanks for this exercise. It is so valuable to me! So important to be reminded that I'm part of a context!
Birgitta

I felt quite bitter when I did this exercise. I reacted to the last question thus, "I have certainly not received anything that has made this possible. I've got to do it all myself!" And in that moment it struck me that the power I've got to do what I am thankful for is from nature, from all my walks in nature, from all the times when I have hugged a tree. Gratitude suddenly filled all of me. Thank you!
Linda

I marvel at how many reasons I find for myself to not "need" appreciation; I'll be the lone warrior, and the lone warrior needs no appreciation. Only when I take time to mourn this do I find gratitude.
Johan

Might work especially well if you have a high score on happiness strategies:
2. (Cultivating optimism)
5. (Nurturing relationships).
11. (Practicing religion and spirituality)

5th Happiness Survey

Fill in the Oxford happiness survey on page 169 and save it in a place where you can easily find it. When you have completed the survey, compare the numbers you came up with earlier with the ones you got now.

Week 23

Appreciating Everything You See

Do this exercise several times during this week; maybe take a moment for it daily. Find a place where you can sit undisturbed for 5 - 10 minutes. It can be indoors or outdoors.

Let your eyes land on any object in your vicinity. Is there something in that object that can stimulate appreciation in you? Is there any gratitude for this item being there? If so, where does the gratitude come from, what needs are met?

There is no need to be in a hurry, you might only look at one particular object for the whole exercise. If you feel like it, you let your eyes wander and look at many things. Use a gratitude journal and write down what you appreciate with this exercise.

After this exercise, I have started to say thank you, sometimes quietly, sometimes out loud. I say thank you during the day when I remember it, when I see beautiful scenery, or when I hang out with people I like. I have started to take every possibility to get this yummy experience. I give thanks, inhale deeply into my heart and enjoy the feeling - feeling myself relax throughout my whole body and letting the gratitude take over. Awesome!
Carola

Might work especially well if you have a high score on happiness strategies:
3. (Avoiding overthinking and social comparison)
9. (Savoring life's joys)
11. (Practicing religion and spirituality)

Week 24

Symbols of Gratitude

Marshall Rosenberg told me that for many years he has written a gratitude journal. He focuses on what he has done that he appreciates but also on what others have done. To really take in the feeling of gratitude he draws a flower while he thinks about what he is thankful for.

So the exercise I am suggesting this week is to focus on what you or anyone else has done that you appreciate, connect it to the needs that were met and what emotions it stimulates. Then draw a symbol or picture while you reflect about the gratitude. It could be a flower, but also something else. Any image or symbol that supports you in taking in and integrating the gratitude will do.

Do the exercise every day or as many times as you want this week. Experiment with the symbol or image that best helps you to bring in the appreciation.

This week's task was fun. I tried to find symbols for things I appreciated. And in that way it became clearer to me as to how many things I appreciate. Although I did not always find a picture or symbol, it gave me inspiration to look for them. Moreover, the picture makes it easier for me to remember the appreciation for a longer time. It was creative, imaginative, humorous and playful. I have longed to come into connection with this joy within me.
　Elisabeth
　Might work especially well if you have a high score on happiness strategies:
　1. (Expressing gratitude)
　8. (Flow)
　9. (Savoring life's joys)

Week 25

Gratitude Album

This exercise is in a way a continuation of last week's exercise since it is also based on images, photos and pictures.

This week's task is to start making an album with images that can help you experience more gratitude. It can be cartoons, photographs of people or places, symbols, or anything else you can put in an album. Let the album grow over time and use it as often as you like to be reminded of things that you are grateful for.

I chose to make a folder on the desktop of my computer. So that I can run slide shows and watch when I want.
    Johan

> Might work especially well if you have a high score on happiness strategies:
> 5. (Nurturing relationships)
> 9. (Savoring life's joys)
> 10. (Committing to your goals)

6th Happiness Survey

Fill in the Oxford happiness survey on page 169 and save it in a place where you can easily find it in four weeks time. When you have completed the survey, compare your numbers with you previous answers.

Week 26

Evaluation – Half Way

This week it's time to reflect. Take time to read through your gratitude journal. Read the notes and other things you've written so far. If this does not suit you, you can repeat any of the previous exercises (see more on that in week 27) or do the exercise for week 28.

Take time to celebrate what you have done so far to experience more happiness and gratitude in your life. Maybe you want to assess, using the questions under week 13, and become more aware of what actually makes you happy every day.

Note at the end of each day some activities the day was filled with. Note also how happy you were during each of these activities (e.g. on a scale of 1-10). Ask yourself if there is anything in particular that helped you feel happy and grateful? Read your notes at the end of the week and make a plan for how you can spend more time on the activities you listed as the most rewarding. You can also let this exercise stretch longer to get a broader overview.

Already after a few days I realized that I spend very little time on things that really make me happy. Time for some major changes in life!
Marianne

Might work especially well if you have a high score on happiness strategies:
8. (Flow)
9. (Savoring life's joys)
10. (Committing to your goals)

Week 27

Choose an Exercise

I hope that last week's reflective evaluation gave you some clues about the types of exercises that are best suited for you so that it is easy to select any of the exercises you have already done and repeat them.

To consciously choose something that enhances our experience of gratitude and our happiness level is in itself an auspicious event. If you want more clarity in what you can choose, reflect on what the Happiness strategy test in chapter 4 showed you and choose in connection to that.

I was surprised that I chose the exercise to express appreciation to others because I have always experienced this as very scary in the past. But it was also the exercise that has affected me the most.
Mats

Might work especially well if you have a high score on happiness strategies:
8. (Flow)
9. (Savoring life's joys)
10. (Committing to your goals)

Week 28

Appreciating the Person You are Today

Think back to an earlier period in your life when you needed support, maybe when you were between 10 and 18 years old. Maybe you longed for another person, a peer or an adult. who could have helped you in some particular way. Take a moment to connect to what need of yours you would have liked to have received support around at that time.

Ask yourself:

In what way am I now the person I would have wanted to meet back then?

How could I now be the support that I was yearning for back then?

How would I have been able to help this young person to support their needs?

Breathe in and give space for the questions. If the answer is not clear, ask yourself again:

What have I learned about life, feelings, needs, love, empathy, honesty, and connection that could support me in connecting with my young self?

Write down things you are grateful for, name what you have received that have brought you to this point.

What have you learned about life, feelings, needs, love, empathy, honesty and human connection that you could share with this person?

How could you be a role model for this person?

Please do this reflection every day for a week or as many times as you feel nurtured by it.

For a number of years in adolescence I was longing for "unconditional love". I would have wanted more support in mourning my mistakes. I would have wanted some empathy. Just typing the word "empathy" evokes sadness, as I cannot recall anything that resembled empathy in my life during those years. I just want to embrace myself and really mourn this.
    Ellen

When I ask myself in what way I am the person I would have liked to meet, I realize how often I listen to young people and use the power of empathy. I do not give sympathy or advice. When I realized that I give the gift of myself and that I would have liked to have had that from someone when I was young, it fills me with gratitude and pride in myself.
    Carola

Might work especially well if you have a high score on happiness strategies:
6. (Developing strategies for coping)
7. (Learn to forgive and listen with empathy)
10. (Committing to your goals)

Week 29

Gestures of Gratitude

Gratitude is felt in the body. It can be stimulated again and again as a never-ending stream. This week I suggest that we find a gesture that makes it even easier for us to celebrate it. Many athletes, such as football players, have a certain gesture that they use to enhance the experience of scoring. Let yourself be inspired by them to find a gesture you can use to enhance your sense of gratitude.

Start by finding a gesture, big or small, that you want to choose as your gesture of gratitude. Then focus on something you feel grateful for. Your notes or diary may be a place for inspiration. Chose something that you very clearly are grateful for, something that really touches you. It could be a memory of something you have done that you appreciate or something that someone else has done that you feel grateful for. Think about the situation or action, take a few deep breaths, let it touch you and then make the gesture that you have chosen. It may be something subtle like a certain smile or something you do with your fingers or something more audible or visible to others.

Do this exercise a few times during this week, preferably five times or more, so that you get the chance to repeat the gesture and it begins to feel natural to you. Notice if this gesture helps you to be more deeply affected by the appreciation and if so, use it for strengthening the exercises in the coming weeks.

I chose to open my hand and then slowly close it again. That symbolizes what gratitude is for me. To open up to what life has to give, and then to embrace and enjoy it.
Birgitta

What worked best for me was that I allowed myself to smile while I focused on gratitude. Sometimes it felt silly, but more and more, it really deepened the experience of gratitude.
Ellen

> Might work especially well if you have a high score on happiness strategies:
> 9. (Savoring life's joys).
> 10. (Committing to your goals)
> 12. (Meditation and taking care of the body)

Week 30

Appreciating a Contemporary Role Model

Express your appreciation to some living individuals for doing things that benefit a larger group of people. Call or write them! It may, for example, be a person who appears in newspapers, television, or someone sitting in municipal government, or someone working for some bigger goals in some association, a politician or a celebrity.

Express appreciation to as many people as possible and notice if this feels fun for you. If you have trouble finding what you appreciate, look around and see what you are thankful for? Maybe there are useful roads? Schools? Efficient public transport? Music? TV programs? How are all of these things contributing to you and to others?

Express what you have seen and heard them do and the needs that have been met by their actions. Express appreciation in a way that you think makes it easy for the recipient to receive it, whether you know for sure that it will reach the person or not. Enjoy the joy of giving.

If you want, you can go one step further and find out the person's email address or postal address. Maybe the person can only be accessed via their website, blog, or equivalent.

> Might work especially well if you have a high score on happiness strategies:
> 1. (Expressing gratitude)
> 2. (Cultivating optimism)
> 10. (Committing to your goals)

7th Happiness Survey

Fill in the Oxford Happiness Survey on page 169 and save it in a place where you can easily find it in four weeks. When you have completed the survey, compare your numbers with the first round if you did it before you started.

Don't miss this great opportunity to get feedback and remember it's not to late to do it now even if you have not filled it in before.

Week 31

Things That Stir Happiness & Joy in Me

Make a list of things that specifically stimulate gratitude and joy in you. They can be people, places or events that particularly affect you and open your heart. Put the list in a place where you can add to it easily during the week. Maybe take a look in your gratitude journal and notes from the past weeks to get inspiration. This list will be used in the exercise practice for the following week, so be sure to save it. Also take some time whenever you like to read it and get inspiration.

Working with appreciation daily gives me an incredible increase in self-awareness and self-esteem.
Linda

Might work especially well if you have a high score on happiness strategies:
1 (Expressing gratitude)
2 (Cultivating optimism)
8 (Flow)
9. Savoring life's joys.
10. Committing to your goals.

Week 32

Heart Connection

Take the gratitude list you wrote in the previous exercise. Make sure to have at least five minutes of undisturbed time to do the following. Read the paragraph that begins on page 166 to get more clarity on this approach. Connect to your heart through the exercise below – inspired by HeartMath exercises as well as by Metta-meditation.

Sit, lie or stand. Keep your eyes open with a soft gaze. Breathe slowly and deeply into the belly. Let your breaths be three to five seconds long. Make the in breath as long as the outbreath. If you breathe in five seconds, breathe out five seconds. Continue breathing in this way and put all your attention on the area around your heart. It can be helpful if you put one hand on the heart. Imagine that you are breathing in and out through the heart.

Once you have found this "heart centered breathing," think of something that touches you (use the list you wrote last week) and allow your heart to be affected. Breathe and continue to focus on the area around your heart. Let your breath and attitude and eyes be soft.

Use 5-10 minutes, preferably every day or more often to do this exercise. Please read more about HeartMath later for inspiration and clarity. If you find it hard to relax with breathing, feel free to stand or walk slowly as you do the exercise.

If you notice that you lose concentration, do the exercise more often but for shorter periods and be sure to have your eyes open. This exercise, like many of the others, loses its power when it is a struggle to do it. In this exercise it is counter-productive to struggle in order to achieve results. It has a more positive effect on your system when you enter a stage of "being" rather than "doing".

One way to help this to happen is to wait for each new moment. There is nothing to rush into, nothing special to achieve. It is more of an invitation to a process than to reach a goal. Here is an excerpt from a dialogue about this in one of the test groups.

When I cannot find concrete things that stimulate my joy, it becomes difficult to get to my heart. Then I started to lay a hand on the heart and it often helps me connect, even without having a certain thing I'm thankful for.
Marianne

This week I have tried to do this exercise with breathing, focusing on the heart and bringing in something that I wrote on the list last week. It is simply not possible. I just get stressed. It's like my body does not want to do it. But I found my own way of doing it. I went out walking while doing the exercise! And then I could really take in what I'm happy about in a completely different way.
Elisabeth

When I come to a soft place inside, I let go of the memory of the appreciation, and focus only on my heart. For me, this is the "whole thing" - to focus on what helps the heart to live and be warm and soft.
Mia

Might work especially well if you have a high score on happiness strategies:
1 (Expressing gratitude)
11 (Practicing religion and spirituality)
12 (Meditation and taking care of the body)

Week 33

HeartMath in Action

1. Start with doing the exercise from week 32 for a while each day or as often as it feels okay. If possible do it just before you take step 2.

2. Express appreciation to at least one person (out loud) and pay attention to your heart when you express it. At the end of the week summarize how this has affected you during the week. Please continue to do the exercise from week 32 in connection with the exercise as often as you can and feel free about doing it.

It's so awesome. Breathing seems to work as some kind of gratitude drill inwards.
Mia

The heart is actually some sort of inner mid-point. That's where all melts and falls into place.
Marianne

Might work especially well if you have a high score on happiness strategies:
1 (Expressing gratitude)
11 (Practicing religion and spirituality)
12 (Meditation and taking care of the body)

Week 34

Places of Gratitude

During this week, I thought that we would explore how different environments can stimulate our gratitude. Therefore do this exercise as many times as possible in different locations. Do it rather for many short moments than to take one long time period for it.

Maybe you want to write down what you find out at the various locations to become even more aware of it. By now you know what to do that will make your gratitude grow, so practice an exercise that works well for you and in the places, indoors or outdoors, that you already know work for you. Or – do something else if you are looking for a challenge.

Allow yourself to experiment with new surroundings and be ready to be surprised! Do the exercise at least one time indoors. Just look around, sit down, walk or stand and take in how you feel the gratitude of what you are experiencing right where you are. If you want, you can use the HeartMath exercise where you breathe with deep regular breaths, focusing on your heart and thinking of something that makes you happy or grateful as described in the two previous weeks.

Do the exercise outdoors at least once. Maybe you will find your own "Gratitude Garden"!

My favorite gratitude places are either in front of the fireplace or in front of the large window facing the garden. But now I have tried new places . . . It was not news to me that I could feel gratitude while in the shower- feeling the water on my skin, but I learnt to use the time sitting on the toilet for a while, for giving thanks, and it was also satisfying. It inspired me to try out even more places – so when I was standing in a long queue in the supermarket I used the time for a gratitude moment. It worked! Now I can enjoy lots of moments that used to be a nuisance!
Birgitta

It's when I'm outside that I feel gratitude most intensely. Being in nature triggers gratitude for the life within me. It's like more of the senses get involved. I can feel the air on my cheeks, hear the drops of water from the roof and experience the smell of the pine needles. All this reminds me of how much I have to be grateful for.
Elisabeth

Might work especially well if you have a high score on happiness strategies:
8 (Flow)
11 (Practicing religion and spirituality)
12 (Meditation and taking care of the body)

Week 35

Gratitude Walk

Take a walk, preferably in an environment where you in the previous exercise noticed that it was easy to experience gratitude. Maybe you want to walk on a beach, in the woods, along a path up a mountain or maybe in a garden or park. Walk slowly and focus continually on your heart. Let the surroundings affect you and let each step be a deliberate step.

Take a walk as many times as you want to during the week and enjoy it as much as possible. The walk can be as short as a few minutes or as long as several hours.

These words of Thich Nat Than help me to understand the power of this exercise and to enjoy it even more.

The mind can go in a thousand directions,
but on this beautiful path, I walk in peace.
With each step, a gentle wind blows.
With each step, a flower blooms.
    -Thich Nath Than[2]

Nature really helps me relax deep into my soul! I am so grateful for the peace it brings.
Lennart

Might work especially well if you have a high score on happiness strategies:
8 (Flow)
11 (Practicing religion and spirituality)
12 (Meditation and taking care of the body)

---

2 *http://www.plumvillage.org/songs-for-the-practice/110-the-mind-can-go-in-a-thousand-of-direction.*

Week 36

Quarterly Evaluation

This week it's time to reflect on the last half year. Take time to read through your gratitude journal, notes, and other things you've written so far. If this does not suit you, you can repeat any of the previous exercises, or do the exercise as described for week 37.

Take time to celebrate what you have done so far to experience more happiness and gratitude in your life. Reflect on what it has given you to focus on gratitude and get more clarity about how you want to precede. Perhaps some of the questions below can be of help.

1. Do you have one or more favorite exercise?

2. Is there any exercise you feel hesitant about or did not get anything out of? What can you learn from it, for example, about what happiness strategies suit you the best?

3. What has helped you to continue doing the exercises?

4. What has made it challenging to keep doing them? Do you see any pattern in this?

Might work especially well if you have a high score on happiness strategies:
2 (Cultivating optimism)
3 (Avoiding comparisons)
8 (Flow)
9. Savoring life's joys.
10. Committing to your goals.

8th Happiness Survey

Fill in the Oxford Happiness Survey on page 169 and save it in a place where you can easily find it in four weeks. When you have completed the survey, compare your numbers with the first round if you did it before you started.

Week 37

Choosing an Exercise

My hope is that last week's reflective evaluation gave you some clues about the type of exercises that are the most rewarding to you, so that it is easy to see which of the exercises you would like to select in the future.

Some of the exercises that I've heard people appreciate doing the most on a regular basis are those that express appreciation for oneself or others, the exercise on doing nothing, and writing in the gratitude journal. Some people like the more challenging ones like asking for gratitude but report that they do not like to do them regularly but more as an occasional challenge for themselves.

> Might work especially well if you have a high score on happiness strategies:
> 2 (Cultivating optimism)
> 3. Avoiding overthinking and social comparison.
> 8 (Flow)
> 9. Savoring life's joys.
> 10. Committing to your goals:

Week 38

Appreciating Your Body

Take a few moments during this week to appreciate your body again. You can sit, stand, lie or walk when you do this exercise. Start with checking how your body feels right now. Focus for a moment on the body parts that feel comfortable. Then connect to your heart. It is beating and beating, minute after minute, hour after hour, day after day, year after year, completely at your service. Ask yourself if this is something you appreciate - the job that the heart does?

Then connect with another body part and think about what that does. Is it something you enjoy that this body part or organ does for you? Is there anything else you want to appreciate your body for?

Avoid "pushing" appreciation by thinking that you "should" be grateful, and more importantly, notice if you are actually experiencing gratitude for your body. Summarize what you have learned at the end of the week.

This was the most difficult exercise for me so far. There was much discontent about my body that showed up during this exercise and I noticed I was trying to avoid focusing on it by not doing the exercise. But the moment I could remember what miracles our bodies are and perform every day, it was super nice. I noticed that I have something to work on here, so I will continue with this exercise for some weeks.
Marianne

Might work especially well if you have a high score on happiness strategies:
9. Savoring life's joys.
11 (Practicing religion and spirituality)
12 (Meditation and taking care of the body)

Week 39

Gratitude for What You Take for Granted

Take a moment early in the week and reflect on things you take for granted, but which you actually feel a lot of gratitude for. Write down what it's about, and as often as possible during the week remind yourself of this. Make a list and read through it every now and then to remind yourself.

Remind yourself as many times as possible during this week about these things. You may decide to do it spontaneously or during a scheduled period in the morning or evening.

For example, give thanks for
- waking up
- being able to open your eyes and stretching. Noticing how it feels when your feet meet the floor for the first time, is there anything that you are grateful for at being able to do this?
- You might want to continue to give thanks for being able to breathe and that there is abundant fresh air for you.
- When you dress, you can be thankful for the way the fabric feels against your skin,
- or for having clothes to put on.
- Maybe you want to connect with your gratitude for being able to hear, see, or move, or for anything else you might take for granted.

I wonder how I could have missed this about so many things. That there was so much to appreciate that I have never seen. I was moved to tears and elevated.
Marianne

After identifying the "obvious" things that I feel gratitude for, I noticed I began to take them less for granted. Taking a moment every morning before I get out of bed to thank life is good for me. It increases my ability to enjoy the rest of the day and also to put up with things that go wrong.

Birgitta

Might work especially well if you have a high score on happiness strategies:
3. Avoiding overthinking and social comparison.
6. Developing strategies for coping
8. (Flow)
11. (Practicing religion and spirituality)

Week 40

Appreciating Role Models

Write down appreciation for someone who you feel has contributed to humanity or to the Earth in a way you are grateful for. It may be someone who is known in the world, or someone more unknown, someone who is dead or still alive. Someone who is a role model for values that you want us all to hold high. Someone whose actions you want to hold high.

Write down what actions you appreciate, what you feel when you think of them and the needs they help you meet. Take your time to really embrace and enjoy this.

Note what happens to you when you do this exercise and allow yourself to really experience the feeling of gratitude. Maybe you want to do this exercise every day and focus on one role model per day (or as often as it feels relaxing) to do so. Write about several role models at one time and maybe extend the list as the week goes by.

I often feel impatient and cannot understand how, for example, Nelson Mandela could endure the stuff he did and still continued to have a belief that things would change. I'm amazed at the clarity and persistency I see in this. I get warm and feel a strong connection to my heart when I think about these people. I do not know if I would call it gratitude but I feel inspired and for that, I am grateful.
   Elisabeth

> Might work especially well if you have a high score on happiness strategies:
> 2. (Cultivating optimism)
> 9. (Savoring life's joys)
> 10. (Committing to your goals)

Week 41

Expressing Appreciation Again and Again

Express at least one appreciation to someone around you every day of this week or express appreciation to several people in a single day if it suits you better. Try to do this at least seven times during the week, but do not force or fake it! The experience is more important than the exercise.

Do it on several occasions and to different people and note how the differences between them affects you. Connect with the people and tell them what you have seen them do or heard him or her say, what you feel when you think about this and what needs are met by it.

Maybe you could also ask the person how it is for him or her to hear your appreciation. Make sure they and you do not expect to feel in any particular way about this. Write a summary of what you have learned at the end of the week - if that is fun for you.

I have noticed that I like to give appreciation a lot and that I get very excited and happy while doing it. What I like the most is to tell someone when he or she has done or said something that touches me and to share that touched feeling with them.

Elisabeth

Might work especially well if you have a high score on happiness strategies:
1. (Expressing gratitude)
4. (Practicing acts of kindness)
5. (Nurturing relationships)
7. Learn to forgive and listen with empathy.

9th Happiness Survey

Fill in the Oxford Happiness Survey on page 169 and save it in a place where you can easily find it in four weeks. When you have completed the survey, compare your numbers with the first round if you did it before you started.

Week 42

Thanking the Senses

Take a moment every day, or as often as you feel like it, where you can be relatively undisturbed (at least not around people that talk to you if possible). Connect to your senses. Your touch, hearing, sight, taste and smell. (If you are deaf, blind or lack taste or smell, simply skip this.) Recognize how this is for you. Then ask yourself if that connection brings up any gratitude in you?

Remember, if you expect certain feelings or expect yourself to feel grateful, it will probably not happen because gratitude blooms in the light of freedom.

This exercise did not do anything for me at first. Then I focused on my ability to see and quietly said the words - "Thanks for being able to see". Then I continued in the same way with the ability to hear - "thanks for being able to hear," and so on. Each time I was filled by a wave of warm gratitude. Realizing how I have been taking this for granted made me even more grateful – this time for the exercise itself.
Linda

Might work especially well if you have a high score on happiness strategies:
2. (Cultivating optimism)
9. Savoring life's joys.
12. (Meditation and taking care of the body)

Week 43

Appreciating your Ancestors

Many cultures and traditions regularly focus on giving thanks to their ancestors. This is done in many different ways and often includes thanking yourself for everything you have received as a result of what the previous generations have achieved. Let us be inspired by them this week.

Do this exercise as many times as you want and in the format that suits you the best. Choose a person who lived before you, it can, for example, be your grandmother, grandfather or even someone further back in time. Then write a letter to this person, or write a speech, a song or a poem. Maybe you want to approach several people in the same letter, or write personal letters to each one. You can start with the observation of something they did or something that someone had heard them say. Then tell them what you feel when you think about it and link it to what needs are nourished by it right now or what values this helps you hold high.

Although there might be things you do not like that these people have done, at this moment you will put your focus on what you do appreciate. Take time to read out loud what you have written and enjoy the gratitude it might help you feel.

I thought the first exercise seemed "airy-fairy." Then I realized that without my ancestors, I would not even be here, and then it was easy to feel gratitude.
Lennart

Might work especially well if you have a high score on happiness strategies:
6. Developing strategies for coping
7. Learn to forgive and listen with empathy.

Week 44

Appreciating Yourself for the Last 24 Hours

Today we are going back to one of the original exercises, because appreciation for ourselves often gives us strength and inspiration. This is a variation. Do this one, or stay with the earlier format.

Take a few moments to write down appreciation for yourself. Choose something you've done in the last 24 hours that you really feel grateful for.

Then connect with the needs that were met by what you did. Also connect with what feeling it stimulates to think about this appreciation. Take your time to let it touch you. Maybe you also want to ask yourself what you have received that has made it possible for you to do this thing that you appreciate. Notice if there is any difference between this week and when you expressed appreciation for yourself before.

There is usually a clear feeling inside me of joy when I'm very concrete in the description of what I appreciate. But sometimes it is not so. Sometimes something really abstract stimulates a really strong feeling of gratitude that I love to stay with.
Mats

Might work especially well if you have a high score on happiness strategies:
3. (Avoiding comparisons)
6. Developing strategies for coping
9. Savoring life's joys.
11. (Practicing religion and spirituality)

Week 45

Doing nothing

Take five minutes each day this week to do nothing. I suggest that you read about Sabbath in Chapter 2 and repeat the instructions for week seven. Write a reflective summary at the end of the week. You might want to focus especially on what happens to your heart and your sense of gratitude when you do nothing.

Might work especially well if you have a high score on happiness strategies:
6. Developing strategies for coping
8. (Flow)
9. Savoring life's joys.
11. (Practicing religion and spirituality)
12. (Meditation and taking care of the body)

Week 46

Expressing Appreciation

Express appreciation to someone in your closest surroundings, as many times as you want to during this week. Maybe you want to aim at one person per day. You can choose to express what you wrote last week or express something else. I suggest that you do it on several occasions and with several people, in order to learn as much as possible about how it affects you to express appreciation.

Connect with the person and tell them what you have seen them do or heard him or her say; what you feel when you think about it, and what needs were met by it. Maybe you also want to ask the person what it is like for him or her to hear your appreciation. It may not be possible at all times to express it directly. In this case you can call or write instead. Write a summary of what you discovered at the end of the week.

> Might work especially well if you have a high score on happiness strategies:
> 1. (Expressing gratitude)
> 4. (Practicing acts of kindness)
> 5. (Nurturing relationships)
> 7. (Learning to forgive and to listen with empathy)

Week 47

Happy Birthday!

Prepare yourself for celebrating someone's birthday. Choose a person you appreciate, someone who is important to you in some way. Write a speech of gratitude for their next birthday (whenever it will be). Perhaps a speech you think you would never give or a speech you would really like to share.

It can also result in a letter that you send on this person's birthday. Do the exercise as many times as you want during the week and write to as many people as you want. Maybe you also want to write one for your own next birthday, and write what you have been especially grateful for in the past year.

Notice how it feels for you to write (and to maybe to give) the speech.

> Might work especially well if you have a high score on happiness strategies:
> 3. Avoiding overthinking and social comparison.
> 4 (Practicing acts of kindness)
> 5 (Nurturing relationships)
> 7. Learn to forgive and listen with empathy.

10 th Happiness Survey

Fill in the Oxford Happiness Survey on page 169 and save it in a place where you can easily find it in four weeks. When you have completed the survey, compare your numbers with rounds before to see if there is any change.

Week 48

Who Wants Appreciation?

Ask at least three people this week if they would like to hear some appreciation from you. Ideally, approach different people, to learn as much as possible. Maybe you want to give all the appreciation in one day or just to one new person each day. Maybe you want to focus on your family, friends or colleagues. Try different ways to ask and if you get a no, consider whether there is anything in your way of asking that can be made more inviting.

Express what you have seen the person do or heard him or her say, what you feel when you think about it and what needs were met by it.

Maybe you also want to ask the person how it is for him or her to hear the appreciation. It may not be possible at all times to express it directly to them. In this case you can maybe call or write. Note what happens inside you, before, during and after you have expressed your appreciation.

Might work especially well if you have a high score on happiness strategies:
3. Avoiding overthinking and social comparison.
4. (Practicing acts of kindness)
5. (Nurturing relationships)
7. Learn to forgive and listen with empathy.

Week 49

Appreciating Yourself

Use some moments each day, or at least three times during this week to focus on appreciation for yourself. You can do it in the way proposed in week 22 or week 44.

Write down something you've done that you really appreciate. It can be something you've done in the last day or something that you did long ago. Big or small does not matter. Then connect with the needs that were met by what you did. Also connect with the feelings thinking about this action stimulates.

Consider whether it suits you best to do this in the morning, in the evening before going to sleep, or at any other time during the day. Write a summary of your reflections at the end of the week.

> Might work especially well if you have a high score on happiness strategies:
> 2 (Cultivating optimism)
> 3. Avoiding overthinking and social comparison.
> 6. Developing strategies for coping.

Week 50

A Future You Are Grateful for

If you find a happy person, you will also find a project.[3]

Describe yourself in a future where everything has gone very well for you; when you have worked hard and succeeded in achieving some of your life goals and dreams. Maybe you want to keep a diary for a few days and build up an image under the line "what I dream of seeing myself doing and experiencing in the future" or "My dream." When the dream is clear, imagine that you are expressing appreciation and gratitude to yourself or to someone else in that situation. What would you say?

As a closing, take a moment and connect with how it feels and the needs that are met. Use a moment every now and then during the week to reconnect to this future dream scenario and to the gratitude it generates. For example, imagine what a typical day or week in your dream life looks like, imagine the way you live or what you do, including what others would say to you and about you.

> *This was a challenging exercise for me! It was not until I tried to describe a concrete dream week in my future that I "got it". Then I felt gratitude and curious anticipation in a heavenly beautiful way.*
> Linda

> Might work especially well if you have a high score on happiness strategies:
> 3. Avoiding overthinking and social comparison.
> 6. Developing strategies for coping.
> 9. Savoring life's joys.
> 10. Committing to your goals.

---

[3] Lyubomirsky, Sonja (2008), The How of Happiness. Penguin.

Week 51

Expanding Your Heart – Appreciating an "Enemy"

This exercise may be seen as a kind of examination. It is about seeing if your heart can generate some appreciation to someone you might normally find it difficult to appreciate. Maybe even someone you see as an enemy or a threat. Choose a person that you do not feel indifferent about, but that you find challenging to appreciate. Focus on something that this person has done or does that has met some need of yours. It may help first to focus on the needs that he or she was trying to meet in a situation, the person's intention, even if the result was hurtful to you or to someone else.

Sometimes it helps to imagine that there is someone who you easily feel appreciation towards doing these things. It can release the action from being tied to the person and that might enable a first step toward gratitude.

I want to do it with as wide and open a heart as I know is possible. I want to stretch my heart muscle, bringing each cell to focus on seeing the intention.
   Johan

> Might work especially well if you have a high score on happiness strategies:
> 4 (Practicing acts of kindness)
> 5 (Nurturing relationships)
> 6. (Developing strategies for coping)
> 7. (Learn to forgive and listen with empathy)

Week 52

Gratitude Speech to the Most Important Person in Your Life

During this week, take time to reflect, read your gratitude journal, notes, and other things you've written this year.

Take time to celebrate what you have done so far to experience more happiness and gratitude in your life. Reflect on what you have received through focusing on gratitude this year and if you want to continue to invite more gratitude in your life in some way. Are there any gratitude exercises you want to continue to do? Maybe you want to take time for things that you have realized bring you happiness, such as meditation, to care for your close relationships, or to tend to "old wounds" with empathy.

A way to end this year of gratitude is to organize a party for yourself where you give a gratitude speech to yourself, full of appreciation! Or a party where you invite others that you give gratitude speeches to, or that you ask to express appreciation to you. Play with it, have fun, express, take in, give away, learn and live!

Might work especially well if you have a high score on happiness strategies:
1 (Expressing Gratitude)
6. (Developing strategies for coping)
9. (Savoring life's joys)
10. (Committing to your goals)

Evaluation and the Last Happiness Survey

Now that you have gone through all the exercises you can fill in the Happiness Survey on page 169 again. Compare your numbers with the other series of surveys you have done. Maybe you want to regularly continue to do this assessment to monitor if you are doing what makes you happy or not.

Also consider whether to continue doing gratitude exercises of some kind. Was there any exercise you skipped that you want to go back to? Some you wanted to deepen and focus on during more than a week? Was there any kind of exercise that affected you strongly that you want to do as long as it is meaningful?

Or maybe you become aware of very different strategies to keep the gratitude fire alive. Something that you want to devote time and energy to, in order to continue to stretch your gratitude muscle. Whatever you do to keep your heart alive, I wish you good luck!

If the Fire of Motivation Fades Away

When I start doing exercises based on how I "should" do them or because I have said that I should do them, or even because I think that it is "good for me" my motivation fades.

After hearing Marshall Rosenberg recommend a gratitude journal, I set an intention to write an appreciation every day. It seemed such a good idea. I bought a beautiful journal and set out for the journey of my life.

After a couple of weeks I lost all joy in doing this and I could hardly put my eyes on the journal without frowning. Every time I saw it I felt I had failed and criticized myself for not having completed what I had set out to do.

When I later encountered Sonja Lyubomirsky's book, I felt a big relief to get more words to describe the connection between variation, free choice and connection when it comes to gratitude.

I had approached my gratitude diary with the attitude that this was going to be "good for me" and "I should do it". This made it as fun as a prolonged dentist appointment. This ambitious but awkward attitude was a threat to my autonomy. And rather than giving me joy, it bored me to my bones.

If you find that your motivation to do the exercises decreases, it may be the result of one of the following. Are you thinking something like:

1. I feel so bored! I just want to get it all over with.

Is it the need for stimulation or perhaps the need for meaning that wants to be taken into consideration? Or is it the need for free choice and to be able to decide for yourself that is speaking to you?

If it is the needs, for example for freedom and meaning, you might ask yourself if you can create more variation in your exercises? Can you create an experience of more autonomy by doing them only once in a while or at times that suit you more than at the times you think are appropriate? Did you do them in ways that give you meaning?

If you find that you have done the exercises out of duty or because it is beneficial or because you feel guilty about not taking control in your life, or because you see it as useful, then take a look at your motivation to do them at all[4]. Maybe the dutiful thoughts are hidden behind seemingly motivational thoughts like "I've decided this so now I have to pursue it."

2. Does this really make sense? What will this give me?

Maybe it is your need for meaning or to experience results that is talking to your through the boredom? If you recognize these kinds of thoughts, one way to manage them is to choose exercises specifically from the happiness strategies that work the best for you. Please go back to your answers to the test in chapter 4 - then carefully choose which of the gratitude exercises you want to do. Remember that you can always skip exercises or do an exercise that you enjoy for a longer period of time. You can get concrete feedback about if you are actually making progress by regularly using the Happiness Survey on page 169.

3. It's not fun to do this alone. I want to do something together with others.

If you experience thoughts such as these, you might be connecting to the needs of community and companionship. Perhaps you have a high score on nurturing relationships in the happiness strategy test on page 76. If this is the case, you can think about strategies that invite others to your gratitude gym. For example you can gather a few interested friends and do exercises together or regularly find some way to share things you have learned with others. Maybe you want to do more exercises that have to do with expressing gratitude to others or asking for appreciation.

Happiness research has shown that if we have other people to repeatedly share gratitude with, it increases our happiness level. Do not hesitate to do only one type of gratitude exercise if they are the

---
4. Larsson, Liv (2012), Anger, Shame and Guilt, Reclaiming Power and Choice. Friare Liv.

only ones that your heart seems to get into.

It was not until I had found myself a "happiness friend" that I felt the exercises really had some effect. When I had someone to share my insights and my celebrations with, they became more real and it became much easier to motivate me to continue.
Marianne.

Wow, I feel full of new information and new exercises. I also find that I am not giving up because it's just too interesting, but it feels as if I'm spinning in a clothes dryer.[5]

If you think and feel this way, maybe it is the need for rest and to integrate which are showing themselves here. If so, it may help to not change exercises as often as I suggest in the book. Another suggestion is to do the exercises "Appreciating your body", "Doing nothing", "Thanks for the Food," "Gratitude Walk" or "Gratitude for the day" for some time or before doing any other exercises. They all include some rest and might meet the need to integrate intense learning and emotions.

Thirty Days Challenge

For those of you who have a tendency to "give up" something you have started or find it difficult to create new habits, try a "Thirty Day Challenge". Choose a strategy that feels fun and natural to you. Decide that you will do everything you can to implement the practice for 30 days. You can choose one of the exercises from the book and keep with that for 30 days. You can also decide to use 5 different exercises or more and make a plan of how many days you will do one or the other or mix them up all together. The most important thing is that you do it during a time span of 30 days.

---

5. One of the people in the "test group" expressed herself above, after 10 weeks of intensive practicing. She decided to stick to the same one exercise for a few weeks instead of changing them so frequency and found her motivation again.

After these 30 days evaluate whether you want to set new goals, finish here, fill in the happiness strategy test, or to do something else inspired by this book.

Which Exercises Suit You Best?

If you do not want to do the exercises in the order presented or have lost motivation, you can use the "crib" below as an aid to see what exercises might suit you the best. Note that this is not a "truth" but you are evaluating how you perceive the exercises and use this as inspiration. The following chart of happiness strategies I have borrowed from the book "How of Happiness".[6] Most of the exercises are suitable for those who have high scores on the first happiness strategy – expressing gratitude.

1. *Expressing gratitude.*
2. *Cultivating optimism.*
3. *Avoiding overthinking and social comparison.*
4. *Practicing acts of kindness.*
5. *Nurturing relationships.*
6. *Developing strategies for coping.*
7. *Learning to forgive and listen with empathy.*
8. *Doing more activities that truly engage you. (Flow)*
9. *Savoring life's joys.*
10. *Committing to your goals.*
11. *Practicing religion and spirituality.*
12. *Taking care of your body.*

---

6. Lyubomirsky, Sonja (2008), The How of Happiness.

Week	Exercise	Happiness Strategy
Week 1	Gratitude Diary	(1, 2, 9, 11)
Week 2	Enjoying Gratitude	(1, 6, 9)
Week 3	Appreciating Somebody Else	(2, 4, 5, 7)
Week 4	Expressing Your Appreciation	(4, 5, 7)
Week 5	Appreciating Yourself	(2, 3, 6, 9)
Week 6	Gratitude Diary	(3, 6, 9, 11)
Week 7	Doing Nothing	(6, 8, 9, 11)
Week 8	Receiving Appreciation	(3, 5, 6, 9)
Week 9	Asking for Appreciation	(3, 5, 6, 9)
Week 10	Thanking the Day	(1, 3 9, 11)
Week 11	Expressing Your Appreciation	(1, 4, 5, 7)
Week 12	Appreciating Yourself	(2, 3, 6, 9)
Week 13	Quarterly Evalution	(3, 8, 9, 10)
Week 14	Choose an exercise	(3, 8, 9, 10)
Week 15	Thanking Your Food!	(1, 9, 11, 12)
Week 16	Need Mediation	(1, 9, 11)
Week 17	Connecting Needs to Gratitude	(8, 9, 11,12)
Week 18	Who Wants Appreciation?	(2, 4, 5)
Week 19	Appreciating Your Body	(9, 11, 12)
Week 20	Emotions as Clues to Gratitude	(8, 9, 12)
Week 21	Expressing Your Appreciation	(1, 4, 5, 7)
Week 22	Your Link in the Chain of Giving and Receiving (5, 7, 11)	
Week 23	Appreciating Everyhing You See	(3, 9, 11)
Week 24	Symbols of Gratitude	(1, 8, 9)
Week 25	Gratitude Album	(5, 9, 10)
Week 26	Evaluation – Half Way Through	(3, 8, 9, 10)
Week 27	Choose an exercise	(3, 8, 9, 10)
Week 28	Appreciating the Person You are Today	(6, 7, 10)
Week 29	Gestures of Gratitude	(9, 10, 12)
Week 30	Appreciating a Contemporary Role Model	(1, 3, 10)
Week 31	Things That Make You Feel Good	(2, 8, 9, 10)
Week 32	Heart Connection	(1, 11, 12)
Week 33	HeartMath in Action	(1, 11, 12)
Week 34	Places of Gratitude	(8, 11, 12)

Week 35	Gratitude Walk	(8, 11, 12)
Week 36	Quarterly Evaluation	(3, 8, 9, 10)
Week 37	Choose an exercise	(3, 8, 9, 10)
Week 38	Appreciating Your Body	(9, 11, 12)
Week 39	Gratitude For What You take for Granted	(3, 6, 8, 11)
Week 40	Appreciating Role Models	(2, 9, 10)
Week 41	Expressing Your Appreciation	(1, 4, 5, 7)
Week 42	Thanking the Senses	(2, 9, 12)
Week 43	Appreciating your Ancestors	(3, 6, 7)
Week 44	Appreciating Yourself	(3, 6, 9)
Week 45	Doing Nothing	(6, 9, 11, 12)
Week 46	Expressing Your Appreciation	(1, 4, 5, 7)
Week 47	Happy Birthday!	(3, 4, 5, 7)
Week 48	Who Wants Appreciation?	(3, 4, 5, 7)
Week 49	Appreciating Yourself	(2, 3, 6, 9)
Week 50	A Future You Are Grateful For	(3, 6, 9, 10)
Week 51	Expanding your Heart	(4, 5, 6, 7)
Week 52	Gratitude to the Most Important Person in Your Life	(3, 6, 9)

Cooperation Between Heart and Brain

I have found the paradox, that if you love until it hurts, there can be no more hurt, only more love .[7]
Mother Theresa of Calcutta

At the HeartMath-Institute in the US, research on how the heart and brain cooperate has been done.[8] It has been discovered that there are certain factors that help create coherence between the signals that go between our brain and our heart. For instance, deep, calm, regular breathing while directing attention to the area around our heart creates connection. It has also been discovered that we may further improve coherence between the heart and brain through focusing on what touches us, what we love and enjoy and are grateful for. Talking about what we want, long for and need rather than about what we do not want or what we are dissatisfied with have proven to make a big difference to many of our physical processes. More than 1000 different chemicals change their flow depending on which of these directions we take in our thinking and communication.

When we focus on gratitude and what we appreciate, our brain sends out some kind of "reward" (chemicals) to the body and asks it to release "feel good hormones", which contributes to a rising level of gratidude.[9] It becomes a virtuous circle where the heart, brain and our nervous system are all affected.

We can see our emotions as a prayer - a prayer for well-being and love that we can carry with us throughout the day. On my first long meditation retreat in Sri Lanka, I learned a meditation that

---

7 20130909. http://www.brainyquote.com/quotes/quotes/m/mothertere142106.html
8. HeartMath Institute is a research institute that focuses on emotions physiology, communication between the heart and brain, neuro-cardiology and stress management. The institute conducts research in basic psycho-physiology, neuro-cardiology and biophysical research, where clinical investigations of functions from workplace and organizational perspective, and treatment are included.
9 For more detailed descriptions of what happens in the body, see www.heartmath.org

I really enjoyed. It was the Buddhist "Metta-mediation". Later in life I learned HeartMath techniques and was happily surprised as I saw a lot of similarities to the Metta – meditation. The Heartmath techniques have a lot of scientific research backing it up. The Metta approach to "praying" has us move from focusing on our thinking, or our brain, to the area around the physical heart.[10] Once we have shifted our attention, we focus our attention on what we wish for others and ourselves. We might put a hand on our heart and remind ourselves that we want to be happy, but also that we enjoy that others are happy as well.

I have often felt it as my heart opening, or cracking. I might feel it as a soft pain, and strangely enough at the same time I'm also filled with a pleasant feeling of warmth and presence.

You can go further and imagine that you breathe in and out through your heart and let gratitude flow in and out of it. Allow the breath to become an affectionate inner caress. To go one step further, you can imagine that people nearby are part of this feeling of gratitude or love. You breathe in and take in this warming feeling and breathe out and imagine that you are sending it out to others. Maybe you want to take even one more step and imagine that you could send this feeling to people who are not close to you, perhaps even to someone you would call an enemy.

Here are some words from people who wrote about their insights after doing the exercises in week 31 - 33.

For my heart to be calibrated, it needs to be vulnerable and open, and therefore I realize it needs lots of trust that there it is cared for. It is in my heart I feel love, empathy, caring and warmth, so I want to take really good care of it.
Birgitta

It is through my heart that I know what belonging is and it gives me information on how I relate to others and can contribute to them.
My heart's vulnerability is its strength.

---
[10] This exercise is called Heath Lock-in by the HearthMath institute. It has many similarities with Buddhist Metta meditation.

*My heart knows how life should be lived.
It is in direct contact with life.*
Linda

Do not ignore seemingly small signals from the heart - they often tell of great things and are important! Be sure to nurture it by listening with warmth and with presence to its beat.
Ellen

Questions and Answers About HearthMath

The exercises from the HeartMath institute feel so simple, can they really be effective?

You can impact the autonomic nervous system that controls 95% of the body's functions by inhaling breaths equal to your exhalations. If you focus on the heart while breathing in this way it will help you achieve coherence, which then affects the rest of the body, including the brain.

Why it is recommended to keep your eyes open when doing HeartMath exercises?

It is recommended to keep your eyes open because these exercises are not about relaxation, but about creating coherence. And if you do the exercises at all times, even when driving a car, you do not want to only be able to do this with your eyes closed. The exercise does not primarily aim to calm yourself or lower your pulse, but is about creating coherence between the heart and brain; it can also be done in high intensity situations such as during physical activities such as running or biking.

But isn't it also about being able to relax? I relax better with my eyes closed.

Of course you can have your eyes closed, if you are not driving a car when you are doing the exercises. But there is an important difference between coherence and relaxation and the purpose of these exercises is primarily to contribute to coherence. Relaxation can be described as slowing down and letting go of tension. Coherence training is getting our heartbeat to be steady, no matter what the pulse beat is, and seeing that "all systems" beat at the same rate and work coherently together.

I have difficulties in connecting with the heart, it feels so unclear to me, what this means?
One suggestion is to keep a hand on the heart area of your chest so you can more clearly feel that area. Another is to stand up and do the exercise so that the area around the heart can be freer. For some, it works best to do the exercise if they slowly walk at the same time.

Oxford Happiness Survey[11]

Feedback providing clarity in how we develop is very valuable. Without feedback we do might not notice the progress we have made. Feedback also means that we get information on when we are not making progress and what, changes we want to make.

In order to measure the changes you make in inviting more gratitude and happiness into your life, use the overview below. Go back to it as often as you want, preferably once a month for a year or so. This scale can be used as a yardstick to monitor how your experience of happiness changes over time. It is comparison with yourself that says something about how strong the impact of your actions are, not comparison with others who take the survey. Let it be the basis of reflection, rather than proof of how something "is".

Below are a number of statements about happiness. Read all three statements in each group in a sequence and choose the one that best describes how you have been feeling the past week, including today. Please indicate how much you agree or disagree with each statement by entering a number alongside it according to the scale below.

---

11 Lyubomirsky, Sonja (2008), The How of Happiness.

1 strongly disagree, 2 moderately disagree, 3 slightly disagree
4 slightly agree, 5 modarately agree, 6 strongly agree.

____ 1. I don't feel particularly pleased with the way I am. (X)
____ 2. I am intensely interested in other people.
____ 3. I feel that life is very rewarding.
____ 4. I have very warm feelings towards almost everyone.
____ 5. I rarely wake up feeling rested. (X)
____ 6. I'm not particularly optimistic about the future. (X)
____ 7. I find most things amusing.
____ 8. I am always committed and involved.
____ 9. Life is good.
____ 10. I don't think that the world is a good place. (X)
____ 11. I laugh a lot.
____ 12. I am well satisfied with everything in my life.
____ 13. I don't think I look attractive. (X)
____ 14. There's a gap between what I would like to do and what I have done. (X)
____ 15. I am very happy.
____ 16. I find beauty in some things.
____ 17. I always have a cheerful effect on others.
____ 18. I can fmd time for everything 1 want to do.
____ 19. I feel that I'm not especially in control of my life. (X)
____ 20. I feel able to take anything on.
____ 21. I feel fully alert.
____ 22. I often experience joy and elation.
____ 23. I don't find it easy to make decisions. (X)
____ 24. I don't have a particular sense of meaning and purpose in my life. (X)
____ 25 . I feel I have a great deal of energy.
____ 26. I usually have a positive influence on events.
____ 27. I don't have fun with other people. (X)
____ 28. I don't feel particularly healthy. (X)
____ 29. I don't have particularly happy memories of the past. (X)

How to calculate your score:

Step 1: The numbers you have choosen the 12 items marked with an X should be "reverse-scored". That is, if you gave yourself a 1, cross it out and change it to a 6; if you gave yourself a 2, change that to a 5; change a 3 to a 4; change a 4 to a 3; change a 5 to a 2; and change a 6 to a 1.

Step 2: Using the changed scores for those 12 items, now add your scores for all the 29 items.

Step 3: Happiness score = Total (from Step 2) ___ divided by 29 = ____

Your total happiness score is ___ . Date: _____
Your total happiness score is ___ . Date: _____
Your total happiness score is ___ . Date: _____
Your total happiness score is ___ . Date: _____
Your total happiness score is ___ . Date: _____
Your total happiness score is ___ . Date: _____

The lowest possible score on the Oxford Happiness Questionnaireis 1 (if you gave yourself a 1 for all 29 items) and the highest possible score is 6 (if you gave yourself a 6 for all 29 items).

Thank You!

I have a lot to be thankful for. During the approximately two years that I have been writing this book, I have received valuable support from many people. Several of them did all the exercises for a year and gave me a lot of invaluable feedback. Some from that group also read what I have written and provided feedback on what could be changed and added. Special thanks to Birgitta Nilsson, Kay Rung, Carola Johansson, Katarina Hoffmann, Belinda Poropudas, Medina Törrisen, Johan Rinman, Jenny Nilsson and Elisabeth Öhman. Thanks also to the many others who have contributed with insight, clarity, inspiration and gratitude.

Here is some of the feedback on the exercises:

"It has led me to feel more joy, love and gratitude in my life, and I feel that I have some control over my life and that what I do matters. I have become more aware of what I have power over and what I do not have power over."
Birgitta

"I have gained more confidence that I can influence myself and others and that life wants the best for me."
Elisabeth

I am grateful that during the writing process my understanding of happiness has increased. Now I can actively create more of it in my own life. It helps me, almost daily, consciously choose some activity that I know will raise my happiness level, and every day I focus for some moments on something that I am grateful for. It takes no extra time but it makes a big difference.

Finally I want to say thanks to my son who every day reminds me that I want to live and live well. He helps to "take me by the collar" when I want to complain instead of doing something to create my own happiness.

Remember that Happiness is no further away than a "thank you"!

Some basic feelings we all have

Amazed	Fulfilled	Joyous	Stimulated
Comfortable	Glad	Moved	Surprised
Confident	Hopeful	Optimistic	Thankful
Eager	Inspired	Proud	Touched
Energetic	Intrigued	Relieved	Trustful
Angry	Discouraged	Hopeless	Overwhelmed
Annoyed	Distressed	Impatient	Puzzled
Concerned	Embarrassed	Irritated	Reluctant
Confused	Frustrated	Lonely	Sad
Disappointed	Helpless	Nervous	Uncomfortable

Some basic needs we all have

Autonomy
- Choosing dreams/goals/values
- Choosing plans for fulfilling one's dreams, goals, values

Celebration
- Celebrating the creation of life and dreams fulfilled
- Celebrating losses: loved ones, dreams, etc. (mourning)

Integrity
- Authenticity • Creativity
- Meaning • Self-worth

Interdependence
- Acceptance • Appreciation
- Closeness • Community
- Consideration
- Contribution to the enrichment of life
- Emotional Safety • Empathy

Physical Nurturance
- Air • Food
- Movement, exercise
- Protection from life-threatening forms of life: viruses, bacteria, insects, predatory animals
- Rest • Sexual expression
- Shelter • Touch • Water

Play
- Fun • Laughter

Spiritual Communion
- Beauty • Harmony
- Inspiration • Order • Peace
- Honesty (the empowering honesty that enables us to learn from our limitations)
- Love • Reassurance
- Respect • Support
- Trust • Understanding

Litterature and References

Bauer, Joachim (2007), Varför jag känner som du känner. Natur&Kultur.

Brown, Brene (2011), Gifts Of Imperfection. Let Go of Who You Think You're Supposed to be and Embrace Who You are. Hazelden Information & Educational Services

Ehrenrich Barbara (2010) Bright-Sided: How Positive Thinking Is Undermining America. Picador.

Frank, Viktor (1980), Man's Search for Meaning. Beacon press.

Holst, Sven-Göran (red.) (2002), En rimligare värld. Libris.

Gibran, Kahlil (2006), The Profeth. Oneworld.

Kohn, Alfie (1999), Punished by Rewards, The Trouble with Gold Stars, Incentive Plans, A's, Praise, and Other Bribes. Houghton Mifflin.

Larsson, Liv (2010), Anger, Guilt and Shame. Reclaiming Power and Choice. Friare Liv

Larsson, Liv (2008), A Helping Hand, Mediation with Nonviolent Communication. Friare Liv.

Liedloff, Jean (2006), The Continuum Concept: In Search Of Happiness Lost. Perseus Books.

Lerner, Michael (2000), Spirit Matters. Hampton Roads Publ. Company.

Lyubomirsky, Sonja (2009), The How of Happiness: A New Approach to Getting the Life You Want. The Penguin Press.

Muller, Wayne (1997), How Then, Shall We Live?: Four Simple Questions That Reveal the Beauty and Meaning of Our Lives. Trade Paper. Bantam. USA.

Muller, Wayne (1999), Sabbath, Restoring the Sacred Rhythm of Rest. Bantam Doubleday Dell.

Rosenberg, Marshall (2007), Nonviolent Communication, a langugae for Life. Puddle Dancer Press.

About the Author

Based in Sweden, Liv Larsson, is a CNVC-certified trainer and mediator. Trained by Marshall Rosenberg, founder of NVC, she has worked internationally sharing leadership, communication and mediation skills since 1992.

Together with Kay Rung, she has translated and published several books by Marshall B. Rosenberg. Her interest in a deeper understanding of the structures built on domination that foster conflicts, has led her to start several year-long educational programs for basic and advanced NVC-skills, mediation etc.

She has written 15 books on NVC, including two for children. Her books, *Anger, Guilt and Shame - Reclaiming Power and Choice, A Helping Hand, Mediation with Nonviolent Communication*, as well as *Relationships, Freedom without Distance, Belonging without Control*. Many of her books have been translated into several other languages.

For more information about Liv's Books: www.livlarsson.com
For more information about Liv's trainings: www.friareliv.se/eng

Books by The Author

Anger, Guilt & Shame
Reciaiming Power and Choice
By Liv Larsson

ISBN: 978-91-979442-8-1
215 pages

Relationships
Freedom without distance
connection without control
By Liv Larsson

ISBN: 978-91-979442-0-5
69 pages

A helping hand
Mediation with Nonviolent
Communication
By Liv Larsson

ISBN: 978-91-976672-7-2
257 pages

For more information about Liv's Books:
www.livlarsson.com

www.ingramcontent.com/pod-product-compliance
Lightning Source LLC
Chambersburg PA
CBHW031254230426
43670CB00005B/181